Happy Without the Meal

Happy Without the Meal

Reflections from Catholic Faith and Reason

WILLIAM J. ELENCHIN

WIPF & STOCK · Eugene, Oregon

HAPPY WITHOUT THE MEAL
Reflections from Catholic Faith and Reason

Copyright © 2013 William J. Elenchin. All rights reserved. Except for brief quotations in critical publications or reviews, no part of this book may be reproduced in any manner without prior written permission from the publisher. Write: Permissions, Wipf and Stock Publishers, 199 W. 8th Ave., Suite 3, Eugene, OR 97401.

Wipf and Stock
An Imprint of Wipf and Stock Publishers
199 W. 8th Ave., Suite 3
Eugene, OR 97401

www.wipfandstock.com

ISBN 13: 978-1-62564-164-9

Manufactured in the U.S.A.

A Big Mac—
the communion wafer of consumption.[1]
—JOHN RALSTON SAUL (1947–)

Contentment is natural wealth;
luxury, artificial poverty.
—SOCRATES (470–399 BC)

---

1. Saul, *Doubter's Companion*, 10.

Contents

Preface *ix*

Acknowledgments *xi*

Introduction 1

One The Stress of Leisure 9

Two The Nature of Things 31

Three The Rise and Fall of Health and Habits 60

Four The Manufacturing of Illness 83

Five The Futility of Fear 97

Six Faith, Freedom, and Fun 107

Bibliography 137

Preface

This book is written for a wide audience, but my inspiration for writing it is an admittedly small group of people: my kids. I enjoy thinking back to being their ages. Great memories of fun, laughter, and getting in some trouble now and again all quickly come to mind. Good, normal stuff my children experience now as well. But if there's one thing that seems to have changed it's that now it appears harder in today's society to see what is real, what's true.

My youngsters, who range from grade school to college age, have grown up amidst an avalanche of marketing and consumerism. On one hand technology has made life much better, from simple conveniences like staying in touch by cell phone to advanced medical procedures that relieve pain and heal illness. On the other hand time honored values and ideals for living have so eroded and been under attack that it's now more difficult to see the path for living a good and happy life.

In the following pages I will touch on some of the many changes that have occurred in society that seem to have brought such cultural confusion. Not the least of which is the notion that we cannot find, or discern truth. My Dad, easily one of the happiest people I've ever known, liked to keep it real by saying, "We're only passing

Preface

through." If life is a journey, then it's probably a good idea to have a map of the terrain, and a compass for direction.

Acknowledgments

I would like to express gratitude to my family and friends for their support and encouragement during this writing project. For me this process felt very much like running a marathon. The challenge made it fun, but at times the effort felt strenuous. My wife Kate and children Zac, Mary-Kate, and Hannah were a constant source of refreshment, never taking any attitude other than *when* the book is finished, never "if." I am in debt to many kind and insightful friends, especially Brad and Jay, whose own debates about wellbeing and purpose were intriguing, and helped to stir my thinking. I also must say "thank you" to my many wonderful colleagues at the university where I teach. From the administration that supported me by granting a writing sabbatical, to my peers whom I've gained so much knowledge and wisdom from. Last, but certainly not least, I want to share my appreciation for the students who I have fun learning with. They are the reason I am one of those lucky ones who gets out of bed and wants to go to work.

Introduction

> Money never made a man happy yet, nor will it. There is nothing in its nature to produce happiness. The more a man has, the more he wants. Instead of its filling a vacuum, it makes one. If it satisfies one want, it doubles and trebles that want another way. That was a true proverb of the wise man, rely upon it; "Better is little with the fear of the Lord, than great treasure, and trouble therewith."
>
> —BENJAMIN FRANKLIN (1706–1790)

This is a simple yet bold statement; a declaration that materialism has *never* made a person happy and never will. Seen through the lens of our present-day culture, the idea is dismissed as outdated. Over the last few centuries our materialistic society has evolved with religious-like zeal into a kind of consumer creed. Products and services satisfy. More is always better. Stuff makes us happy.

In these words Franklin also speaks of there being nothing in the "nature" of prosperity that leads to happiness. Nature suggests self-evident principles or wisdom, available to all, which can serve to guide a good life. Today his words seem archaic, naïve, and above all, unsophisticated. This is in part because the notion that folks can figure out how to flourish and live well appears to be fading.

A Cultural View of Happiness

Franklin's timeless words from over two hundred years ago help set the twofold purpose of this book. The first is to uncover the subtle but powerful social forces that appear to be having a harmful impact upon society. There's an almost continual and conflicting bombardment of messaging that declares to be the holy grail of health and happiness. Yet, like seawater, the more we consume the thirstier, and less healthy, we become.

We also seem to be losing the sense and understanding of what constitutes a good life, which is the second goal of this work. Unquestionably we live in a technologically advanced society. Food, communication, transportation, and education are more accessible and abundant than at any other point in history. From a practical standpoint, life is technically "easier" than ever before. At the same time, ironically, increasing numbers of people are sad and anxious. This period we live in is marked by paradox. Life-giving and satisfying principles are being traded for glittering, but cheap, energy zapping pleasures.

My goal in writing this book is to shine light on some of the key social changes that over time have created a toxic cultural atmosphere in the midst of material abundance. Like a cloudy day, the cultural environment we

Introduction

find ourselves in can limit our vision. At the same time, we have the ability to adjust to the weather by coming in out of the rain, or soaking up summer warmth when the sun shines. We can learn a great deal from nature, even though there is very little "new" in her.

We have an insatiable appetite for pleasures and individual rights, yet there is such loneliness and sadness in our land. We seem to be experiencing what French sociologist Emile Durkheim described over one hundred years ago as *anomie*. Anomie is a condition where there is a breakdown in traditional social bonds that keep individuals, families, communities, and society together. A limitation of this book is that I will not attempt to discuss all of the social factors that have led to this growing sense of alienation, but limit the focus to cultural perceptions of happiness and wellbeing.

Faith and Reason United

> Reason itself is a matter of faith.[1]
> —G. K. CHESTERTON (1874–1936)

In these pages I will draw upon ideas supported by both reason and faith. I teach sociology courses at St. Bonaventure University in New York. Higher education has evolved in such a manner where science and religion are oftentimes deemed to be incompatible. However, the idea that faith and science are two unrelated entities has emerged only during this past century and has become

---

1. Chesterton, "Suicide of Thought," line 34.

quite prevalent. Today it is often considered an established truth.

Parker Palmer is a renowned author and scholar who has written extensively on educational courage and the need for reform in higher education. He argues that our universities have devolved from teaching the whole person—mind, heart, and spirit—into dry information factories where meaning, purpose, and vitality among students and faculty is largely lost.

> Religion and spirituality must be understood as critical parts of the human "mess" that higher education should help students engage. Excluding religion and spirituality from serious study in secular settings is a stunning form of irrationality in itself. Religion and spiritualty are among the major drivers of contemporary life (as one can readily see in any daily newspaper) and of any historical epoch one can name.[2]

In this book "reason" will take the form of academic research and scholarly writings. In other words, research in the social sciences is making new and important discoveries that at the same time have been embedded in Christianity and literature for over two millennia. Both point toward the same true north regarding principles of wellbeing and happiness.

One contemporary example of this can be found in the impressive 2004 academic work titled *Character Strengths and Virtues: A Handbook and Classification.*[3]

---

2. Palmer and Zajonc, *Heart of Higher Education*, 47. Internal quotes, parentheses, and italics within all footnoted material is in the original unless otherwise noted.

3. Peterson and Seligman, *Character Strengths.*

Introduction

Lead authors Martin Seligman and Chris Peterson distill six personality traits that have been scientifically shown to correspond with high levels of emotional health and happiness—wisdom and knowledge, courage, humanity, justice, temperance, and transcendence. The authors point out that these same strengths align with St. Thomas Aquinas' seven heavenly virtues—wisdom, courage, justice, temperance, faith, hope, and love—which were presented *over nine hundred years ago*.

The idea here is that there do exist ways of being that lead to not only an absence of illness, but also to flourishing lives. Living in a culture saturated with the noise of marketing and materialism increasingly mutes these truths. It's important to state early on that today "virtues" often have a stigma attached to them. They are associated with being "good." And good is boring. But what the virtues refer to are really ways of living a full life, a flourishing life. Flourishing refers to a way of being marked by positives such as success, competence, and health. Flourishing lives are fun lives. That's not to say that buying and using stuff isn't fun. Sure it is. But living large, with purpose and meaning, takes "fun" to the next level. The famous writer and Christian apologist C. S. Lewis paints a portrait of this:

> It would seem that Our Lord finds our desires not too strong, but too weak. We are half-hearted creatures, fooling about with drink and sex and ambition when infinite joy is offered us, like an ignorant child who wants to go on making mud pies in a slum because he cannot imagine what is meant by the offer of a holiday at the sea. We are far too easily pleased.[4]

4. C. S. Lewis, *Weight of Glory*, 1–2.

Happy Without the Meal

This book is written with a focus on youth. By "youth" I am not necessarily pointing to the early years in one's life. Childhood is a time of natural energy and enthusiasm for the simplest things. Kids have bright spirits. Everything is new to them. They love to have fun! Young people seem to flow through each day, not weighed down by past mistakes or worries about tomorrow. But more so by "youth" I mean this free, detached way of being. Seeing and joining in life with wonder. These qualities are not restricted by chronological age. We can all bring to mind "old" people we've known whose spirits were light; or those "young" in age that seem worn and tired.

This work is also written from a Christian and Catholic perspective. Catholic literally means universal or far-reaching. Catholicism has a very open, freeing feeling to it. Working in higher education I am very familiar with the hypersensitivity that often accompanies writing or speaking about matters of faith as they relate to reason. The words of St. Thomas Aquinas, *"To one who has faith, no explanation is necessary. To one without faith, no explanation is possible,"* resonate strongly with me. My reason for writing this book is to look under the hood, so to speak, of what has become a massive marketing engine that has transformed consumption into a kind of religion. During the past several decades our culture has become increasingly secular, placing ever-greater focus on self-satisfaction and instant gratification. Progress and plenty can be good things. But with choices come consequences.

More hazardous however has been the messaging, oftentimes in the name of "science," that products and consumption create health and happiness. On one hand the rampant growth of a materialistic worldview poses a

Introduction

challenge to living with faith. Relativism, the belief that no real, authentic truths exist, now competes as its own form of religion within society. On the other hand modern secularism has progressed and shown its full colors, offering a way of being that is bloated and lifeless.

What not only inspires but intrigues me is the cultural shift we're experiencing in understanding what it means to live a good and happy life. There seems to be a tremendous amount of fear and anxiety in our society. This is matched by a seemingly endless number of "experts" who host TV shows, give seminars, develop products, and write books on how to be "happy." But it seems that the more advice and products people consume the less joyful they become.

As a sociology instructor at a Catholic university I am fortunate to teach courses related to how society impacts health, a subject that I'm fascinated with. The changes that have occurred over time stand out so dramatically to me because of the contrasting example of my parents. The famous medical missionary and talented musician, philosopher-theologian Albert Schweitzer (1875–1965) noted that "example is not the main thing in influencing others. It's the only thing."

Both of my parents were born in the early 1920s and lived through the Great Depression. Neither went beyond a high school education. My father was stationed in India with the Army during World War II. Together they had seven children (my younger sister died at birth) and raised six kids on my dad's very modest salary. My mom never learned how to drive a car and worked part time in a clothing factory. They never owned a cell phone, computer, iPod, or new car.

Happy Without the Meal

In spite of their very humble standard of living they were easily among the sanest, brightest, and happiest people I have ever met. I fully admit my bias in favor of my folks. But what stands out is that they were somehow able to live incredibly dignified and joyful lives without taking college classes, reading books about happiness, taking psychotropic medications, or being able to afford luxuries. In fact, by today's standard of living they would be considered poor. They must have had something else going for them.

THE FULL STORY

This book is divided into six sections. The first is titled "The Stress of Leisure" and challenges the notion that we can't have too much of a good thing. The second chapter comments on the importance of considering the natural law as it relates to knowledge as well as a reflection upon how we can know what is real in today's culture. The third section takes a brief look at the history of health, and how our perception of medicine has changed dramatically during the past century. The fourth part exposes the sad reality that while we've seen wonderful medical advancements in our lifetime there's also a dark side to health care where illnesses and disorders have been manufactured. In chapter five we take a look at the delicate, stark reality we will all share in one day: our mortality. The limitations imposed on us by our humanity can help us, perhaps ironically, to live life to the fullest. The final chapter is an offering of seven suggestions for living light in a culture marked by the weightiness of consumption.

One

The Stress of Leisure

> We give up leisure in order that we may have leisure, just as we go to war in order that we may have peace.
>
> —Aristotle (384–322 BC)

We live in a time unlike any other. Modern life is increasingly being experienced through the lens of consumption. Feasting, eating, drinking, and playing have existed throughout history of course, but also being balanced by the naturally opposing traits of fasting, hunger, thirst, and work. A major shift is occurring. Products and pleasure have begun to take the place of purpose in life, and now often give meaning to a person's very existence.

Marketers have long ceased to promote the central function of their products. There is just too much competition for our next burger, soft drink, pair of jeans, and cell phone. The message now is not about merchandise but *happiness.* The products differ, but the ads remain the same. Getting, using, buying, and doing will satisfy us.

The individual and societal impact of overconsumption is destructive. Perhaps the most obvious example is overeating, which naturally causes excessive body weight. Carrying too much body fat can lead to a wide range of health problems, including high blood pressure, type 2 diabetes, high cholesterol, low self-image, and eating disorders, to list just a few. An established gauge to assess reasonably balanced body weight in relation to height is the body mass index, or BMI. We can calculate our BMI by dividing our weight by our height in inches squared, and then multiplying that number by 703. For most people a healthy BMI falls between 18 and 25. Overweight is a BMI from 25 to 29. Obesity is the BMI category from 30 to 40 with extreme obesity being 40 or greater.

Our nation is over-consuming food and becoming fat. The Centers for Disease Control and Prevention (CDCP) reports that adult obesity has risen from a level of 23 percent in the late 1980s, to its current mark of about 36 percent, or that one out of every three grown-ups is obese. An additional 33 percent of adults are classified as overweight, with 6 percent experiencing extreme obesity.[1] This means that *seven out of ten* adults in the United States carry too much body weight.

The problem of food overconsumption is even more alarming for our youth since metabolism slows and weight gain tends to increase with age. The CDCP finds that in children between the ages of two and five, obesity has *doubled* to reach 10 percent while the rate among six- to eleven-year-olds has *tripled* from 7 percent to just shy

1. Fryar et al., "Prevalence of Overweight," lines 1–6.

The Stress of Leisure

of 20 percent between 1980 and 2008. For teens between twelve and nineteen, obesity has more than tripled from 5 to 18 percent during that same timeframe.[2]

Why the increase? Is it because human beings have physiologically evolved and now require more calories to live? Or is it because we're increasingly called upon to perform manual labor and need more food to fuel our energy levels? No. Our physical makeup has not changed since our grandparents were our age and fewer of us are making a living off the sweat of our brow.

The primary cause of the current obesity epidemic can be traced to culturally manipulated ways of thinking (*or perhaps not thinking*) about food. Food is now marketed primarily as a source of happiness, not nutrition. The fast food industry has intentionally marketed what we commonly refer to as "fast food," largely considered to be artificially enhanced but tasty products that are loaded with fat and calories. They do so of course because much more money can be made from processed than from fresh foods. In addition, chemically enhanced products last a whole lot longer than fresh nourishment.

Here marketing plays a critically important role. Corporations spend *thirty times* more to advertise preserved products than they do fresh foods. The billions of dollars spent on food advertisements have proven to be a huge success. In 1970 Americans spent about 25 percent of our food budget eating out. By 1996 that figure had risen to 40 percent. Now we spend roughly half of our food budget outside the home.[3]

---

2. Ogden and Carroll, "Prevalence of Obesity Among Children," lines 8–10.

3. Weitz, "Social Sources," 17–47.

Happy Without the Meal

Interestingly the serving size for typical fast foods such as soda, fries, and burgers has increased in like manner. When sharing this information with my students I use a simple visual aid. I pass around a "small" McDonald's French Fries bag, which was the "regular" and only size that could be purchased when I was a college student in the early 1980s. The small white and red paper pouch is now dwarfed by the regular cardboard containers offered today.

Simply put, if a person consumes more calories than she or he burns off through physical activities, excess fat will be stored in the body. But our consumer culture sends the message that we can have our proverbial cake and eat it too. There are countless weight-loss programs selling the idea that a pill, liquid, technique, or pre-meal bar will negate that natural effect of consuming more calories than are burned off through movement and exercise. But such gimmicks just don't work.

Research findings that were published in the *American Journal of Preventive Medicine* tell us that the secret to successful weight loss is simple, though not necessarily easy. Based on responses from a large national sample of people, eating less food and exercising more were found to be the most effective way to lose weight. In contrast, "Liquid diets, nonprescription diet pills, and popular diets had no association with successful weight loss."[4] None! But why don't these products work? It seems that many are confusing being overweight or obese as a strictly genetic illness, like Crohn's disease or cancer. That weight is somehow separate from the actual process of,

4. Nicklas et al., "Successful Weight Loss," 481.

The Stress of Leisure

well, eating. The authors of this study point to an irony—that participants in programs that require them to eat certain weight-loss products are actually *less* likely to lose weight. The researchers point out that people likely eat too much of these weight-loss products due to the mistaken belief that they are nutritious and contain few calories.

We're teased with the promise of happiness by supersized value meals and then turn to a $50 billion weight-loss industry that blatantly manipulates consumers for profit.[5] Being overweight, caused by overeating, is physical and therefore visual. We know when we've gained weight by experiencing a larger waistline, tighter fitting clothes, and elevated numbers on our bathroom scales. Emotional and psychological overconsumption typically shows no such obvious signs. But while these effects can be subtler, they're at the same time no less damaging.

The Cost of a Lost Perspective

In the small town where I live we're fortunate to have a young and energetic priest who leads our parish community. In virtually every sermon he begins with a joke or story that helps folks connect with the gospel message for that particular day. As I was scratching out an outline for this book he told a parable about a goose that struck a powerful nerve in me. The story went like this:

> A certain goose enjoyed making yearly flights south to warmer climates during the winter months, then would return back north for the summer season. One year he was flying over a

5. Freedhoff and Sharma, "Lose 40 pounds," 367.

barnyard midway through his trip south, and spotted plenty of feed, all free for the taking. He broke from his companions, landed by the food and began to eat freely. He decided to take in the comfort and nutrition, waiting to join his flock on their return flight north. When those six months passed, he heard the air horn like "honk" of his flock as they soared overhead. Excitedly the goose began to flap his wings to rejoin his friends. With strained effort due to the extra weight from feasting he began to rise. He thought for a moment he could catch the group, but soon realized they were well out of sight. The goose decided to go back to the barnyard and rest again until next winter. When that time came he heard the flock overhead, flapped his wings and rose, but this time not as high. The same cycle repeated itself for a few more seasons until the goose finally felt hopeless and gave up even trying. The lure of comfort took away his very nature, the purpose he was made for.[6]

This parable speaks to the hidden trap many fall into during periods of great prosperity, such as the times we live in. Social commentators often point out that we are living through the greatest economic crises since the Great Depression of 1929. But, perhaps we're living through the greatest *perspective* crises since that time as well. In 2012 the unemployment rate hovered between 8 and 9 percent. Between 1933 and 1934 the jobless rate was as high as 25 percent, or one in four Americans out of work. It wasn't until the outbreak of World War II that the unemployment rate fell below 10 percent.

6. Campbell, "Parable of a Goose."

The Stress of Leisure

In fact the standard of living in our nation has risen exponentially since the early part of the last century. The first car affordable to the middle class, Henry Ford's Model T, rolled off the assembly line in 1908. Prior to this time most people traveled by either walking or horse-drawn coach. The first transcontinental phone call was made in 1915. From New York, Alexander Graham Bell, inventor of the phone, called his assistant Thomas Watson who was in California. It wasn't until the 1930s that quick-frozen foods such as vegetables, fruits, and meats were sold to the public. Another nine years passed before General Electric developed the first refrigerator with separate sections for frozen and fresh food, now common to every kitchen.

In the 1940s only 55 percent of homes had indoor plumbing, making life considerably less convenient than today. People commonly used a small shack outside the home, known as an "outhouse," which served as a crude bathroom. There were shortages of all kinds of everyday necessities due to the war effort. "Victory gardens," or small gardens planted in backyards and local parks supplied 40 percent of vegetables to the home front.[7] By 1945 fewer than seven thousand working TV sets were produced with tiny five-inch black and white screens. There were only nine TV stations on air in the entire country; New York City had three, Los Angeles and Chicago each had two, while Philadelphia and Schenectady, New York had one each.[8] Life expectancy was sixty-four years of age, fourteen years below the current level.[9]

7. Lone Star College, "American Cultural History."
8. High-Tech, "History of Film."
9. Lone Star College, "American Cultural History."

Happy Without the Meal

Around the time I was born in 1963 the average American ate 144 pounds of poultry or meat per year. That figure ballooned to 190 pounds by 1999. Drinking water from a bottle instead of the tap has become normal only in the last few decades, yet by 2009 we downed eight and one-half million gallons of bottled water.[10] Cell phones were not readily available and popular until the early 1980s and have of course become commonplace. In fact, as of 2011 the number of mobile devices, 327 million, has exceeded the number of people living in the United States. The use of such devices has exploded. The average household of 2.6 people typically own twenty-four devices, at least one of those being a smartphone.[11]

In 2003 we reached a point where we owned more cars than we had licensed drivers. In 2002 our new homes were 38 percent larger than those built in 1975, in spite of the fact that people were having fewer children.[12] The list could go on and on. The reality is that for most of us not only are our basic needs met, but what would have been for our grandparents "luxuries" have become for us "necessities." More than a half century ago, G. K. Chesterton recognized this emerging cultural trend:

> Comforts that were rare among our forefathers are now multiplied in factories and handed out wholesale; and indeed, nobody nowadays, so long as he is content to go without air, space, quiet, decency and good manners, need be with-

---

10. Bloch, "Fast Facts—Consumption," lines 27–28, 79–80.
11. Kang, "Number of Cellphones," lines 1–21.
12. Worldwatch, "State of Consumption," lines 50–51.

The Stress of Leisure

out anything whatever that he wants; or at least a
reasonably cheap imitation of it.[13]

Along with an explosive shift in individual luxuries came a societal and national spending mindset. The idea of being in debt, owing money, had traditionally been seen as a negative. The common adage "never a lender nor borrower be" now seems to have lost its charm.

Credit cards at gas stations and hotels have been in use since the 1920s, but it's been only since the 1950s that they've become increasingly popular. It wasn't until 1958 that American Express offered its first credit card. Visa, originally Bank of America, began services that same year. Computerization during the 1970s and 1980s enabled credit card companies to more aggressively target "revolvers," people who carry high balances but tend to pay the minimum due on their credit card bills, leading to perpetual interest fees.[14]

Using forceful and shrewd marketing such companies have been able to amass enormous profits on interest payments. They've done this by "normalizing" paying additional money for interest charges in addition to the principle, or original cost for the product or service. For example, say we purchase a computer for $1,000.00. We pay for it with a credit card that charges 20 percent interest. We decide to make monthly payments for five years. At the end of that time we will have paid a total of $1,469.40 for the computer, increasing the original cost by one-third.

---

13. American Chesterton Society, "Quotations of G. K. Chesterton" lines 110–14.

14. Stephey, "Brief History."

Happy Without the Meal

The same mindset exists on a national scope. In the United States the $100 bill is the largest note in circulation. Ten thousand $100 bills equals $1 million. One million dollars is a one followed by six zeros: $1,000,000. A billion dollars equals $1,000 million. That's a one followed by nine zeros. In 1940 the national debt was $43,000,000,000.

By 1980 that figure had risen to $900 billion, or $900,000,000,000. By the new millennia the number reached five and one-half trillion. A trillion dollars is $1,000 billion. At the year 2,000 our national debt was $5,500,000,000,000. By 2012 the national debt had bloated to $16,000,000,000,000.[15] For most people, me included, numbers of this size are impenetrable; they lose their meaning.

These kinds of numbers are so large and inflated they seem not even real, more like Monopoly money. The same can be said for the vast array of communication devices and readily available food and entertainment options. They are in one way great advancements, while at the same time they're culturally pervasive, having seeped into the social fabric. We seem to have entered a point in time where overabundance has led to overconsumption and overconsumption to a sort of cultural lethargy, like feeling sleepy after a big meal.

The idea that more "stuff" buys happiness is a myth that continues to saturate our nation. Consumerism has now morphed into an ideology, a kind of creed, a religion. The belief that meaning and happiness can be found in luxury, ease, and pleasures. This is certainly not a new

15. United States Government, "Federal Debt."

The Stress of Leisure

cultural phenomenon. Writers and scholars have recognized this for many decades.

In 1985 Neil Postman's book, aptly titled *Amusing Ourselves to Death*, details how our society has become intoxicated with the trivial pursuit of meaningless media messaging, confusing our minds and souls. For some time now, like Pavlov's dogs, we salivate when hearing the church bells ringing out from our tablets, smart phones, iPod's, and TV and computer screens. Thirty years ago Postman saw how technology had so saturated our psyche as to become its own creed, system of faith. He writes:

> [Technology] is an ideology nonetheless, for it imposes a way of life, a set of relationships among people and ideas, about which there is no consensus, no discussion, and no opposition. Only compliance. Public consciousness has not yet assimilated the point that technology is an ideology. This, in spite of the fact that before our very eyes technology has altered every aspect in America during the past eighty years. . . . But it is much later in the game now, and ignorance of the score is inexcusable. To be unaware that technology comes equipped with a program for social change, to maintain that technology is neutral, to make the assumption that technology is always a friend to culture is, at this late hour, stupidity plain and simple.[16]

Herein lays the danger. We are swayed to place our happiness in the hands of the latest gadgets, fads, and fashions, all of which change with time. Trappist monk and social commentator Thomas Merton recognized this tendency when writing, "If we are fools enough to remain

16. Postman, *Amusing Ourselves*, 157.

at the mercy of the people who want to sell us happiness, it will be impossible for us ever to be content with anything. . . . The last thing the salesman wants is for the buyer to become content."[17]

Reality Check: Are We What We Buy?

> *"But you don't understand how much stress we're under,"* he said. *"We have classes, need to study, spend time with our friends, worry about money . . . it's hard doing it all."*
>
> *"Okay, let's break that down a bit,"* I replied. *"Let's chat about something you just mentioned that we all enjoy—friendships. One of the rather dramatic changes I've noticed during the last few years of teaching is that so many students seem almost obsessed with checking their cell phones, even during a fifty-minute class."*
>
> *"Well . . . our generation is different from yours. We can multitask now,"* was his response.
>
> *"Good for you,"* I said, *"but from what I'm seeing, at least through non-verbal body language, is that those students often look either anxious or sad. Any thoughts?"*
>
> *"Maybe it's because these things are expensive . . . we need to get our money's worth,"* he offered with affirming laughter from the other students.
>
> *"I've no doubt about that,"* I replied. *"In fact I carry a cell phone, but with the basic plan. I couldn't imagine the cost of something like a blackberry plus a plan, especially for someone still in college. If I may ask, how much do you pay a month?"*

---

17. Merton, *Conjectures*, 98.

The Stress of Leisure

> He smiled awkwardly, mumbled a bit, and said, *"I'm not sure. I'm on my parent's plan."*
>
> I opened the question to the entire class of twenty-three by first asking, *"Does anyone not carry a cell phone?"* No hands went up. *"Then who can tell me what you pay monthly for your service?"* was my next question, assuming at least some students would have that information. They all began to look at one another with a confused expression and again more mumbling. Not one student in class, all ranging between eighteen and twenty-two years of age, had any idea of what their phone service really cost.
>
> Then one young man, a normally quiet baseball player on the university team, who was sitting near the back of class spoke out as if a bright light suddenly went on in his mind. *"That's amazing!"* he said. *"A lot of us are seniors, including me, and we will be on our own paying our own bills in a few months . . . and we don't even know what our cell phones actually cost!"*[18]

I share this story from a spring 2009 Sociology of Health and Illness class to highlight a few points. First to set the tone for the subtle theme of this book . . . being real. We live in a time where overconsumption has saturated our culture to the point of becoming the norm. Never have people so deeply self-identified with consumer goods nor been so influenced by marketing. Countless products such as cell phones that until recently were either considered a luxury or had not even been developed have now become *necessities*. The result is troubling. For many, the blind embrace of "anything new" because it's the latest

18. This discussion took place in my Sociology 420: Sociology of Health and Illness class, spring semester 2009, at St. Bonaventure University, New York.

thing, has had intensely negative physical, mental, and spiritual consequences.

Another purpose for detailing the class discussion is to foreshadow the fine distinction that is necessary in order to understand "relativism." Relativism refers to the idea that there are no absolute truths we can anchor our lives by, or supports to "hang our hat on" so to speak. Truth is individually created. Ethics are not based on principles, but opinion. By its very nature, relativism is insidious, being both subtle and dangerous at the same time. Typically innocent truths at times coexist with disturbing hidden agendas.

For example, corporate marketers would have us believe that technology equates with happiness. The more devices we have the happier we'll become. Yet while the Internet, cell phones calls, and texts are excellent communication tools, social science research reveals the irony that overuse of these communication devices, meant to enhance relationships and wellbeing, often correlate with high levels of stress, sleep problems, depression, and a lower sense of being connected with others.[19]

A final reason to relay the cell phone story from class is that it also connects with the struggles many young people face who've only known material abundance. To say that I enjoy teaching at a small Catholic college would be a large understatement. Teaching, sharing ideas, and pursuing wisdom with young adults is inherently fun. Yet too often have I seen seventeen- to twenty-three-year-olds drained of their enthusiasm and zest for life not because of the demands of academic rigor, but due to an obsession

---

19. Jenaro et al., "Problematic Internet," 309–20.

The Stress of Leisure

with amusement and passing pleasures. This is sad to witness. The teachings of the Christian faith are anchored in a natural joy and freedom, peace and strength. The cheap counterfeits of these virtues are passed off as pleasure and license in an ever-expanding culture of consumption.

> The gospel preached during every television show is, "You only go around once in life, so get all the gusto you can." It is a statement about theology; it is a statement about beer.
>
> It's lousy beer and even worse theology.[20]
> —John Silber (1926–2012)

We are living in a time of paradox marked by contradictions and confusion. We live in a society that, on one hand, has virtually unlimited access to endless varieties of food, clothing, transportation, and instantaneous communication. In addition to these "essentials" and because of exponential technological advancements, we have both more leisure time and entertainment options than any other period in all of human history. Yet in spite of such abundance, so many of us are sad. Anxiety threatens to take hold of our culture, like a dark cloud blocking the light of day. In fact depression has become so established within our culture that we are now deemed to be living "in an era of melancholy" in the midst of material abundance.[21]

Shouldn't constant amusement, pleasure, and ease equate with lasting happiness? Many would think so. On

---

20. Talbot, "Ethics in the Corporate World," 28.
21. Peterson et al., *Learned Helplessness*, 208.

Happy Without the Meal

a surface level it makes sense. There is nothing wrong with having fun. Play, at every age, is good for the spirit, body, and mind. Arguing against basic pleasures would be like questioning the need of fresh air, food, and water, basic elements of survival. The very word "recreation" is the compound of "re-create," meaning to enliven and start anew. The related term "rejuvenates" means to make young again, implying the strength and vitality of youth, adolescence, or early adulthood. But these terms also contain the prefix "re," suggesting a returning to or from something, not a constant state of some fixed activity but more of a balance between rest and effort, work and play.

From a societal perspective, it is not difficult to make the argument that the emergence of a consumptive culture marked by ever-aggressive marketing campaigns has served to warp ideals of health and happiness. By consumptive culture I mean the usually unspoken but collective belief that foods, products, name brands, entertainment, and pleasures alone lead to lasting happiness. One of the more interesting effects of this worldview is that an all-consuming focus on fun dictates, by default, that work, hardships, and challenges are considered meaningless, to be avoided at all costs. Indeed, being challenged and overcoming adversity, once a noble trait, is now often perceived as a detriment to life.

These are the underpinnings of so much contemporary unhappiness. Not only is effort necessary to enjoy rest, but the belief that human beings can somehow escape suffering by consuming things is flawed thinking, which must naturally lead to poor psychological health and harmful consequences.

The Stress of Leisure

No one needs a college degree to recognize the endless examples of product marketing that promise the world. Look around. What do we see on TV, cell phone apps, and the Internet? If we look closely at the messaging we'll most often find that the sales pitch has little to do with the simple purpose of the item, but with making us feel emotionally connected to the product. This is largely due to the fact that we live in such an affluent society. Even those considered "poor" experience relative poverty. This is a form of poverty where people have less material goods relative or in comparison to others in the community. The vast majority who live under the poverty line in the United States still have their basic needs of clothing, food, and shelter met. This is in contrast to absolute poverty found in less developed nations, where people struggle to live without clean water, food, and permanent shelter.

The point here is that the United States and most industrialized nations produce an almost endless quantity of material goods, which makes it extremely difficult to market and sell products based solely on their function or usefulness. Soap is no longer just soap; water no longer water. Shoes are no longer shoes. Imagine walking into a shoe store to purchase a pair of athletic footwear, such as Nike, Reebok, Adidas, Asics, Puma, Brooks, Converse, or my son's favorite, Under Armour, with the labels removed. Corporations have long understood the need to employ psychology in marketing, to tap into a belief that we're connected somehow to the goods or services. The goal is to morph an intimate connection between the person and product, a process known as "branding."

Happy Without the Meal

While marketers do target specific demographic classifications, such as adolescents, college students, urbanites, senior citizens, males or females, their eyes are on a bigger prize. Their goal is to create lifelong, cradle-to-grave customers. Such aspirations necessitate that advertisements first focus on the youngest and most vulnerable in society: little children. The messaging that comes across to kids is simple: "stuff" will make you happy. Materialistic values now challenge traditional values. When materialism wins out, the result is often what one would expect from any form of overconsumption. The natural consequences of obesity, sexualization, and poor emotional development are now self-evident in our society.

A national coalition of educators, health professionals, parents, and advocacy groups, known as the Campaign for a Commercial-Free Childhood (CCFC), reports that marketing costs to children rose from $100 million in 1983 to its current level of $17 billion annually. Products are marketed through all available media. Youngsters between the ages of two and eleven see in excess of 25,000 advertisements yearly just watching television. These ads are effective. Youth below the age of fourteen spend roughly $40 billion per year on products, with teenagers spending $159 billion. All this is quite a sum of money when we consider that the typical teenager may bring home modest part-time pay, if any at all. This generation is also the most branded ever. Thirteen- to seventeen-year-old teens have 145 conversations related to brand products on a weekly basis, which is double the rate of adults.[22]

22. Campaign for a Commercial-Free, "Marketing to Children."

The Stress of Leisure

Marketers have become conniving in their approach, developing an intentional dialogue with children so as to bypass parental oversight.[23] Some of their tactics are the use of popular cartoon figures and films, such as Winnie the Pooh or Shrek to promote fast food. They will often connect food with competition and prizes, conveniently available on their company websites. Seemingly innocent children's websites often have promotions embedded in them. For example the popular virtual pet site "Neopets" has had games that featured McDonald's and Pepsi brands.

Such marketing tactics have largely been spearheaded by the fast food and entertainment industries. In his probing book *Fast Food Nation*, Eric Schlosser exposes how commercial marketing has changed our nation's food consumption and very culture. Schlosser explains the manner in which children are targeted:

> The growth in children's advertising has been driven by efforts to increase not just current, but also future, consumption. Hoping that nostalgic childhood memories of a brand will lead to a lifetime of purchases, companies now plan "cradle-to-grave" advertising strategies. They have come to believe what Ray Kroc and Walt Disney realized long ago—a person's "brand loyalty" may begin as early as the age of two. Indeed, market research has found that children often recognize a brand logo before they can recognize their own name.[24]

---

23. Davis, "Marketing of Foods."
24. Schlosser, *Fast Food Nation*, 43.

Happy Without the Meal

While marketers often begin by targeting children, no age is immune for the consumption onslaught. Advertisers have fine-tuned the art of identifying hot-button emotional issues that range across the life span. The particular emotions may vary, depending on what stage of life we are in. Young children will be tempted with newness, adolescents with excitement, young adults with adventure, and wage earners with increasing pleasure and avoidance of discomfort. But the two-sided coin that draws all of these into one theme are the opposing forces of happiness and fear.

It is of course quite natural and healthy to desire joy and resist pain. But it is equally unhealthy, and in fact highly dysfunctional, to believe that it is not natural for there to be times in life where hurts and sufferings occur, or that each moment of one's existence must be "fun." Yet this imbalanced worldview has seeped into popular culture, taking root during the past several decades and now is in full bloom.

Never Enough Stuff

For many individuals and families the negative effect of a consumptive culture has been devastating. In Greek mythology there is the story of Tantalus. Though only mortal, he is given special privilege to party with Zeus and the other gods, feasting on the best food and drink. He has everything he could want at his fingertips that Mount Olympus could offer. Lacking gratitude and suffering from an inflated ego, he betrays his celestial friends. He steals food and even murders his own son, feeding him

The Stress of Leisure

to the gods to test their divine powers of insight. The tale of Tantalus is best known for the punishment he receives. His eternal fate is to stand chest deep in a cool river with fresh fruit within his grasp, just a few feet above his head. But when he bends over to drink, the water instantly dries up leaving only mud, and when he reaches for the fruit, a burst of wind takes it just beyond his reach. Though surrounded by nourishment, Tantalus can never satisfy his thirst and hunger.

We too are also tantalized dozens, if not hundreds of times daily in a culture driven by image and instant pleasure, and we constantly thirst for more. Part of the genius of the marketing industry has been the subtle nature of the messaging used. There are no imperial troops forcing us to make any purchases, whether for food, clothes, homes, cars, cell phones, or computers. Although the message has been subtle, it has been effective. Buying stuff will make us happy. Economists Hamilton and Denniss detail how pervasive our consumptive culture has become, to the point of constructing a new meaning of happiness.

> Our marketing culture has done something profound right under our noses: it has redefined happiness itself. In place of the time-honored belief that a happy life is one of fulfillment acquired through developing our capacities, cultivating personal relationships and adhering to a moral code, people today have been persuaded that a happy life is one in which we maximize the number of episodes of emotional and physical pleasure, however fleeting they might be.[25]

---

25. Hamilton and Denniss, *Affluenza*, 47.

Happy Without the Meal

The problem with this "new" definition of happiness is simply that it doesn't work. Living for fun alone and to get more and more things just doesn't satisfy. As much as we may want it to, it can't bring happiness, joy, and contentment. Not necessarily because of some moral code, but because of our human nature.

Two

The Nature of Things

> It is impossible for us to break the law.
> We can only break ourselves against the law.[1]
> —Cecil B. DeMille (1881–1959)

The natural law, in a broad sense, refers to a philosophy for understanding how to live a good life. This law, or set of governing principles, gives us the ability to distinguish between actions that are positive as opposed to those that are negative. This way of knowing has been commented on throughout recorded history, from the days of Aristotle to the present. Being philosophical in nature is difficult to sum up in a simple definition. Thomas Aquinas, in bringing together the importance of faith and reason, defines the natural law as "nothing other than the light of understanding placed in us by God; through it we know what we must do and what we must avoid."[2]

---

1. DeMille, Commencement Address, Brigham Young University, May 31, 1957.

2. *Catechism of the Catholic Church*, 475.

Happy Without the Meal

The natural law guiding behaviors, while not as self-evident, still mirrors the natural laws of the physical sciences. Objective truths exist. If a person momentarily holds a pencil between their fingers and then lets it go, the law of gravity will show its presence as the instrument falls to the floor. When a child eats a snack of two cookies and then sneaks in one more, we know with certainty that she or he had a total of three treats, not two or four. Should a scuba diver remain submerged once oxygen has been depleted, survival matters little on their opinion of physiology.

Although philosophically deep, the essence of the natural law confirms that human beings have the capacity to determine what is right and wrong, healthy and unhealthy. We are able to recognize what makes up a good life. There are natural principles that exist throughout history and cannot be changed. Murder is wrong. Parents spending time with their children is good.

In his book *Mere Christianity*, famed Oxford scholar and wounded World War I veteran C. S. Lewis teases out what the natural law means:

> This law was called the Law of Nature because people thought that every one knew it by nature and did not need to be taught it. They did not mean, of course, that you might not find an odd individual here and there who did not know it, just as you find a few people who are color blind or have no ear for a tune. But taking the race as a whole, they thought that the human idea of decent behaviour was obvious to every one. And I believe they were right. If they were not, then all the things we said about the war were nonsense. What was the sense in saying the enemy were

in the wrong unless Right is a real thing which the Nazis at bottom knew as well as we did and ought to have practiced?[3]

Lewis makes the insightful point that we can see the natural law play out even among those who argue that no such principles exist:

> The most remarkable thing is this. Whenever you find a man who says he does not believe in a real Right and Wrong, you will find the same man going back on this a moment later. He may break his promise to you, but if you try breaking one to him he will be complaining "it's not fair" ... It seems, then, we are forced to believe in a real Right and Wrong. People may be sometimes mistaken about them, just as people sometimes get their sums wrong; but they are not a matter of mere taste and opinion any more than the multiplication table.[4]

Thomas Merton offers a similar description of what Lewis called the "Law of Nature":

> The plainest summary of all the natural law is: to treat other men as if they were men ... Everything that is demanded of me, in order that I may treat every other man effectively as a human being "is willed for me by god under the natural law." Whether or not I find the formula satisfactory, it is obvious that I cannot live a truly human life if I consistently disobey this fundamental principle.[5]

---

3. C. S. Lewis, *Mere Christianity*, 5–6.

4. Ibid., 6–7.

5. Merton, *New Seeds*, 76.

Happy Without the Meal

Here Merton points out that the natural law is a "principle," or set of rules that are in place in the cosmos, just like those from the hard sciences touched on earlier. He is clear that it matters not if we agree with them (in his words "find the formula satisfactory"[6]) and cautions that regularly dismissing this reality will result in an undignified way of being.

This same theme is seen again in the famous letter written by Martin Luther King Jr. that was composed during his imprisonment in the Birmingham City Jail in 1963. Dr. King was responding to criticism he received for his equal rights leadership and demonstrations as being "unwise and untimely." In his letter King lays out a reasoned and eloquent response. He acknowledges a valid concern raised by his critics, that being King's willingness to *break* certain laws. But he then goes on to make the critically important distinction between just and unjust laws.

King fully acknowledges the paradox that on one hand he has fought for and supports equal rights legislation, such as the 1954 Supreme Court decision that made segregation in public schools unconstitutional and therefore illegal. Yet on the other hand he has just violated a city ordinance prohibiting public parading without a permit, which led to his arrest. Here King draws upon the natural law to support his reasoning, and begins by paraphrasing St. Thomas Aquinas, pointing out that an unjust law is no law at all. King then continues:

> How does one determine when a law is just or unjust? A just law is a man-made code that squares with the moral law or the law of God.

6. Ibid.

> An unjust law is a code that is out of harmony
> with the moral law. To put it in the terms of Saint
> Thomas Aquinas, an unjust law is a human law
> that is not rooted in eternal and natural law.[7]

The natural law tells us that objective truths exist. That certain ways of being led to health and happiness while other ways lead to illness and sorrow. However, the natural law is seen by many social commentators and scholars to be no longer relevant. Natural law is often deemed to be some outdated concept that ought to have been left in the Middle Ages, before the Age of Enlightenment and progress. Many now embrace the notion that science alone holds the answers to life challenges, and ridicule the notion that there are also rational, natural ways to successfully and gratefully navigate through life.

Blind, Lame, and Stupid

Albert Einstein (1879-1955) is reported to have said, "Science without religion is lame. Religion without science is blind." These words are powerful. They imply a balance between faith and reason. But more than that, they infer recognition that either one when taken to extremes leads to the rather severe handicaps of being without sight or having limited flexibility. There are three important thoughts to consider regarding the science and religion debate, and the first two draw upon Einstein's words.

---

7. King, "Letter from Birmingham Jail," lines 117-20.

Happy Without the Meal

Religion without Science Is Blind

In every age there have been extremists on both sides of this debate, from strict secularists who deem religion as mere myth to religious zealots who are skeptical of science and its advancements. However most of history is not marked by this separation. Universities themselves developed in large part due to the support of various kings and the papacy beginning around AD 1100. And religious scholars have long embraced the search for God by better understanding how the natural world operates. Over time these ways of knowing came to be categorized in distinct academic disciplines, such as geology, physics, history, and philosophy.

Nicholas Steno who was ordained as a Catholic priest in 1675 and as a bishop in 1677, was considered both religious and a man of science, and is known as the father of geology. Bishop of Lincoln from 1235 to 1253, Robert Grosseteste made remarkable scientific contributions during the Middle Ages. His work with mathematics is credited as being a forerunner to establishing scientific explanations regarding nature. The more famous Franciscan friar Roger Bacon, being influenced by Grosseteste, placed great emphasis on the study of nature through the use of experimental reasoning.

Fifteenth-century Catholic cardinal and astronomer Nicholas of Cusa argued that a truly educated person knows how limited his or her knowledge is and defended the notion of an infinite universe. Nicholas Copernicus, Johannes Kepler, and Isaac Newton were heliocentric cosmologists, establishing the sun and not the earth at the center of the universe. All of these great figures believed

The Nature of Things

discoveries about the natural world helped to reveal a living God in nature. Nineteenth-century Augustinian monk and Austrian scientist Gregor Mendel is known as the father of modern genetics.

Author of *Modern Physics and Ancient Faith* Stephen Barr, gets to the heart of the supposed conflict between religion and science by making the case that, in a literal sense, no such war exists. He points not only to the historical record touched on above, but also shows how modern scientific discoveries (e.g., quantum physics and the big bang theory) support a religious worldview.

However Barr does point out that there most certainly is a battle taking place. But the struggle is between religion and materialism. Science is commonly confused with materialism. Science is about empirical findings and hard data, while materialism is a philosophic outlook on life, much like religion. Barr writes:

> The conflict is not between religion and science, it is between religion and materialism. Materialism is a philosophical opinion that is closely connected with science. It grew up alongside of science, and many people have a hard time distinguishing it from science. But it is not science. It is merely a philosophical opinion. And not all scientists share it by any means. In fact, there seem to be more scientists who are religious than who are materialists.[8]

---

8. Barr, *Modern Physics*, 1.

Happy Without the Meal

Science without Religion Is Lame

This notion calls into question the belief that science alone will answer life's riddles and solve its problems. Such thinking is itself unscientific for several reasons. First, scientific findings can only literally be found or "proven" by those who conduct an experiment and establish empirical facts. Researchers are the only ones who have firsthand knowledge of the procedures and results of specific studies. These findings are shared primarily in academic journal articles and are reviewed by other experts within the same subject areas. However those who read and accept scientific knowledge must necessarily accept on good faith the work of their peers, unless they are to replicate the research study themselves.

Second, in the hard sciences, such as chemistry or physics, replication does not create much of a problem since "facts" can typically be verified by conducting an experiment in a research lab. These experiments can then be repeated with precision, establishing validity, or truth. However in the social sciences, such as history, political science, and psychology it is much more difficult, and often impossible, to establish fact (in research this is termed causation). Humanity and behaviors cannot be decoded through a lab experiment. In addition it is not at all uncommon for research findings to contradict one another.

For example, until recently the majority of research on families found that couples without children were happier than those with kids at home. These "findings" have become entrenched in popular media portrayal of families as well. The data seemed to suggest that loss of personal freedoms, additional expenses, and increased responsibility made youngsters a drain on parents' feelings of happiness. I've read these studies for years and always scratched my head because my own experience has been just the opposite.

I married my wife just before turning thirty. While I've been very fortunate in life and was certainly happy before having a son at the age of thirty-two followed by two daughters at thirty-five and thirty-nine, nothing has been as joyful as seeing our kids grow up and being a part of their lives. There are of course the additional responsibilities, loss of free time, and added costs compared to being single. Personal sacrifices have been made to be sure, however that doesn't detract from the experience but is just part of it. But even the "costs" of having and raising youngsters pale in comparison to the abundant joy, humor, and love they've added to our lives.

Now more recent findings published in 2012 contradict previous research and media claims that couples without kids are happier than those with children. The researchers used a combination of three studies. The first was to test how happy parents are compared to non-parents, the second how both groups felt on a daily basis, and lastly how parents rate child-care experiences compared to other actions. The authors found that "contrary to previous reports, parents (and especially fathers) report relatively higher levels of happiness, positive emotion, and meaning in life."[9] They conclude their research report with what would be, for many, a less than stunning revelation:

---

9. Nelson et al., "Defense of Parenthood," 3.

Happy Without the Meal

> Contrary to repeated scholarly and media pronouncements, people may find solace that parenthood and child care may actually be linked to feelings of happiness and meaning in life.[10]

New findings contradict old, supporting time-honored beliefs and, quite honestly, just common sense.

And lastly, the notion that any person can live their life based on the certitude of scientific findings is just silly. It would be impossible to make it through even one day. In fact we'd be hard pressed to go just a few minutes empirically confirming that our toothpaste really contains fluoride and morning cup of coffee is made from actual Arabica beans. As mortal beings we can't state with certainty that we'll even have a tomorrow to wake up to and face. Added to that the inexhaustible list of daily activities we don't directly control.

Stopping for our morning cup of coffee and breakfast sandwich on our way to work we trust that the ingredients are safe and nutritious. When reading the latest news, we place faith in reporters (to some degree) as it would be impossible to personally verify not only world events but even most local happenings. On our drive home from work or school we have confidence that our vehicle will slow as we press the break pad down. Or at least we hope so.

In the fall of 2011 my then fifteen-year-old son was hurt playing in a Friday night football game. The following Tuesday he had a doctor's appointment to assess the damage. On our way there, about five miles from our home, a truck just ahead of us put on his left turn sig-

10. Ibid.

The Nature of Things

nal. I applied my brakes to slow down and immediately felt both alarm and an adrenaline rush as my foot felt no resistance and went straight to the floor. My brake fluid lines had blown! A car was approaching from the passing lane, which left the only option of veering right near a stand of trees. After knocking down several plastic reflectors I was able to dodge the accident, swing back onto the road, and apply the emergency break. Other than frazzled nerves no one was injured.

I have a great automobile mechanic who's an even better friend, whom I have complete trust in. But even advanced technologies, impressive as they are, simply can't be the panacea many hope it to be. Even from an empirical, scientific perspective, virtually all of our days are based on trusting in what we don't personally control. This so-called debate between religion and science breaks down at the most practical level. In his article "Man the Religious Animal," Notre Dame sociology professor Christian Smith speaks to this writing:

> All human beings are believers, not knowers who know with certitude. Everything we know is grounded on presupposed beliefs that cannot be verified with more fundamental proof or certainty that provides us assurance that they are true. That is just as true for atheists as for religious adherents. The quest for foundationalist certainty, with which we are all familiar, is a distinctly modern project, one launched as a response to the instabilities and uncertainties of early-modern Europe. But that modern project has failed. There is no universal, rational foundation upon which indubitably certain knowl-

edge can be built. All human knowing is built on believing. That is the human condition.[11]

Stupidity and Humility in Higher Education

A final thought regarding the supposed battle between faith and science is the consideration of the massive breadth of information that is produced within the educational industry. Human knowledge, let alone supernatural knowledge, is eons beyond the scope and mastery of any one person. In the academe, the primary way to share knowledge is through scholarly journal articles and books. However, working in higher education, it is not uncommon to come across those who take their titles a bit too seriously.

Only after earning my PhD did I fully realize how much I do not and cannot know. Going back just twenty years I can remember visiting the library and pulling index cards to find hardcopy, printed journal articles to read for my studies. With technology, now the availability of information is instantaneous and vast. This is a wonderful tool for efficiency as well as perspective.

It is quite literally impossible to read everything produced in one area of study. As an example Academic Search Complete is a commonly used multidisciplinary academic search engine. It contains more than 7,300 academic journals. These journals are typically published four times per year. Each of these journals contains somewhere between ten and twenty original research articles, review articles, or book reviews. Academic Search

---

11. Smith, "Man the Religious Animal," 30.

The Nature of Things

Complete is one of several dozens of scholarly search engines.

My realization of the vast expanse of literature that exists dawned on me during my studies. With it came a very freeing feeling and balanced perspective. People can be dedicated and work very hard but never possibly master every detail within their fields of study. This also helped me to realize that no one can come anywhere near consuming all human knowledge, let alone declare ultimate truths negating the supernatural realm.

We cannot help but to take much of life on faith in ourselves and in others whom we trust. Microbiologist Martin Schwartz in his humbly titled article, "The Importance of Stupidity in Scientific Research" makes a similar point. His article helps to dispel the false belief that highly educated people have, or are even capable of obtaining complete knowledge. Reflecting upon his own experience he writes:

> A Ph.D., in which you have to do a research project, is a whole different thing. For me, it was a daunting task. How could I possibly frame the questions that would lead to significant discoveries; design and interpret an experiment so that the conclusions were absolutely convincing; foresee difficulties and see ways around them, or, failing that, solve them when they occurred? My Ph.D. project was somewhat interdisciplinary and, for a while, whenever I ran into a problem, I pestered the faculty in my department who were experts in the various disciplines that I needed. I remember the day when Henry Taube (who won the Nobel Prize two years later) told me he didn't know how to solve the problem I was having in his area. I

> was a third-year graduate student and I figured that Taube knew about 1000 times more than I did (conservative estimate). If he didn't have the answer, nobody did. That's when it hit me: nobody did.... The crucial lesson was that the scope of things I didn't know wasn't merely vast: it was, for all practical purposes, infinite. That realization, instead of being discouraging, was liberating. If our ignorance is infinite, the only possible course of action is to muddle through as best we can.[12]

The Atrophy of Higher Education

It is interesting that there is such a high degree of antagonism and at times outright distain toward religion in many universities, since universities developed primarily during the Middle Ages and were largely sponsored by religious and state leaders. These early European institutions were chiefly sponsored by kings or popes. Christopher Lucas, in writing on the history of education, describes how the earliest universities developed from cathedral church schools. He points out that by the end of the seventh century until the eleventh century most of Europe had deteriorated. With the fall of the Roman Empire, so fell cities, maintained roads, monuments, literature, and most anything resembling culture and learning. Competing hordes made almost continual warfare while peasants struggled mightily just to survive. Times were bad. As Lucas writes, "The long night of the Dark Ages had fallen."[13]

12. Schwartz, "Importance of Stupidity," 1771.
13. Lucas, *American Higher Education*, 35.

The Nature of Things

Around the eleventh century life in medieval Europe began to improve. Civilization began to take root once again as cities and towns emerged, agricultural techniques improved, and people organized for civics, industry, and learning. Just beginning to emerge from the Dark Ages, there was little in the way of structured learning. Very few people had the opportunity to receive what we now recognize as an *education*. In 1079 Pope Gregory VII issued a proclamation that schools were to be open in every church cathedral. Here "masters" taught their students not only religious doctrine, but also seven liberal arts—grammar, rhetoric, dialectic, arithmetic, music, geometry, and astronomy.

Lucas points out that cathedral church schools developed into universities in part due to the change in theology being studied as a unique, separate area of learning and scholasticism. Scholasticism is a method of learning where discussion and reasoning are used to defend a position or resolve contradiction. Basically scholasticism took the form of presenting reasoned arguments to arrive at understandings of truth, perhaps most famously seen in the writings of Thomas Aquinas. Lucas makes the point that basically:

> The medieval university as an institution of higher learning grew out of the more advanced courses of instruction evolving within the cathedral church school. What it provided, essentially, was an organized meeting place for students and masters drawn together by a common interest in learning.[14]

---

14. Ibid., 41.

Happy Without the Meal

In fact much of our modern terminology in higher education can be traced back to cathedral church schools. *Discipulorum* is the forerunner of the modern term "academic disciplines," and refers to a group of people interested in learning. Any place where people gathered was referred to as a stadium or "place of study." However it took several hundred years later, around the fifteenth century, when "stadium" was replaced by the current term and idea of what a "university" implies.[15]

The University of Bologna in Italy stakes claim to being the first European university, established in 1088, some four hundred years before the end of the Middle Ages. The University of Oxford is credited as the oldest university in the English speaking world, and was founded in 1096. Its motto is *Dominus Illuminatio Meus*. These are the opening words from Psalm 27, "the Lord is my light." Harvard University, originally a school to train clergy, was founded in 1636, making it the oldest college in the United States. Today Harvard's motto is *Veritas*, the Latin term meaning "truth." However at the time of its founding Harvard's motto was *Veritas pro Christo et Ecclesia*, meaning not just truth, but "Truth for Christ and Church."

Here in the United States the number of colleges had reached nine by the time of the American Revolution. These include Harvard, William and Mary, Yale, University of Pennsylvania, Princeton, Columbia, Brown, Rutgers, and Dartmouth. Most of these schools followed the model set by Harvard, whose ideals in turn followed European universities. These schools were affiliated

---

15. Ibid.

with or sponsored by religious organizations. Harvard, William and Mary, and Yale were founded primarily to prepare young men for Christian ministry. While these institutions have advanced in a more contemporary educational direction, at the time they encouraged a more holistic—mind, spirit, and body—development of the learner.

An example of this is Benjamin Franklin's famous short work *Proposals Relating to the Education of Youth in Pensilvania*, which was written in 1749 and led to the founding of the University of Pennsylvania. Here he lays down core principles for healthy youth development, part of which reads:

> That to keep them in health, and to strengthen and render active their bodies, they be frequently exercis'd in running, leaping, wrestling, and swimming ... Morality, by descanting and making continual observations on the causes of the rise or fall of any man's character ... mention'd in history; the advantages of Temperance, Order, Frugality, Industry, Perseverance, ... Indeed the general natural tendency of reading good history, must be, to fix in the minds of youth deep impressions of the beauty and usefulness of virtue of all kinds.[16]

St. Bonaventure University, where I teach, is a small Catholic school in New York that was founded in 1858 on this same holistic set of values. Bonaventure himself was a Franciscan friar who joined the order in 1243, seventeen years after the death of St. Francis. Bonaventure was highly educated and taught at the University of Paris.

---

16. Franklin, "Proposals Relating to the Education," lines 42–43, 70–72.

Happy Without the Meal

Like St. Francis, he believed that pursuing knowledge for its own sake was vain. The university follows that tradition, summed up in the Bonaventure adage, "we pursue knowledge for the sake of truth."[17]

This idea of "truth" has come under a great deal of assault during the past century in higher education. There has been a strong shift away from developing the whole person toward only recognizing the intellect, and an even further reduction to earning a "grade" and "degree." An increasingly secular approach is now the norm, placing ever lessening emphasis on meaning, values, character, and engagement, which oftentimes leaves the actual process of teaching and learning uninspired and, quite simply, boring.

A key reason for this aridness in the academy is the very powerful shift toward a postmodernism worldview. Post, meaning after the modern period in history. Postmodern is one of those umbrella terms that may be interpreted in various ways, and so defies a simple definition. Theorists who promote this view use language that is rather aloof. Postmodern is a philosophy that suggests that life can be better understood as the mirror-opposite of the modern conception of reality. At its core is the belief that we've reached a point in history where we know that we can't know anything for sure. Truth is relative, meaning realness depends upon a person's subjective, individual experiences. There is no objective reality.

To understand what is meant by postmodern it may be helpful to describe the more easily defined term "modernity." Modernity began with the rise of positivism, or

17. St. Bonaventure University, "Franciscan Values."

the development and use of the "scientific method" that occurred in the shadows of the Enlightenment, which began in Europe around the seventeenth century. The Oxford dictionary describes the scientific method as "a method or procedure that has characterized natural science since the seventeenth century, consisting in systematic observation, measurement, and experiment, and the formulation, testing, and modification of hypotheses."[18] These methods and procedures are more commonly referred to as scientific research.

The Enlightenment marked a shift from knowledge based upon faith and authority toward reliance upon what could be "proven" in both the natural and social sciences. Through the application of research methodology we've experienced tremendous gains in virtually all industries, such as health care, technology, and agriculture. This has led to the notion that continued advances in fields such as chemistry, physics, biology, medicine, economics, psychology, and sociology would steadily improve individual and social wellbeing. While innumerable advances have been realized through research, the many individual and collective problems that remain (and many have intensified) is evidence to its limitations.

Postmodernism, or postmodern thinking, is largely a rejection of modernism. It is more of an intellectual posturing, or theoretical worldview than an established set of ideals. Postmodernist writers, such as Michel Foucault and Jacques Derrida, believe that knowledge is heavily influenced by those who hold power in society,

18. Oxford Dictionaries, s.v. "scientific method," accessed June 3, 2013, http://oxforddictionaries.com/us/definition/american_english/scientific-method?q=scientific+method.

and those with power change over time, making truth flexible and subjective. The sister of postmodernism is "deconstruction," which refers to the practice of breaking down things such as texts, beliefs, and traditions, to reveal their true meaning. The idea here is that words and texts do not, and cannot reveal objective meaning or "truth." What passes for truth is better understood as the opinion a person forms from his or her experiences.

Postmodernism and deconstructionism are very difficult concepts to understand precisely because they are a reaction against what most people recognize as "modern" thought, or the idea that we can acquire knowledge from our own or others' observations; that we can find meaning in life, and discern what is "true." William Grassie, in his scholarly article "Postmodernism: What One Needs to Know," makes the point that "deconstruction, which might be presented as an extreme form of postmodernism, is explicitly an antidefinition theory of thought. So my attempts to define these terms are necessarily self-defeating."[19]

Jacques Derrida, considered the father of deconstruction, has written over forty books and taught deconstruction in universities, extensively in Europe but also in America, until his death in 2004. Because words represented symbols or experiences with no universal meaning, his own explanation of deconstruction is rather muddled. Derrida writes, "Needless to say, one more time, deconstruction, if there is such a thing, takes place as the experience of the impossible."[20] Mitchell Stephens,

19. Grassie, "Postmodernism," 84.
20. Stephens, "Jacques Derrida," line 8.

in a *New York Times Magazine* article reflects on Derrida's perplexing work:

> Although he is often accused of being an apostle of meaninglessness, what is truly disturbing about Derrida is that he finds too much meaning lurking in the roots, etymologies, connotations and sounds of words. His readings focus on these excesses of meaning and the ways the points we are trying to make invariably get tangled up in them, leading to contradictions and misunderstandings.[21]

Stephens makes the important point that Derrida's work has had a large impact on colleges and universities, and quotes conservative critic Roger Kimball who claims Derrida "has helped foster a sort of anemic nihilism, which has given imprimaturs to squads of imitators who no longer feel that what they are engaged in is a search for truth, who would find that notion risible."[22]

In his book *The Hollow Men: Politics and Corruption in Higher Education*, author Charles Sykes takes a position similar to Stephens. Sykes describes the politicization of higher education including the negative fallout that results from deconstructing academia. He writes that deconstruction questions "the foundations of reason and language, arguing that a work of literature—or a 'text' in the obligatory new jargon—was made up of words with no objective meaning, except as reflection of themselves. A narrative thus signifies nothing."[23] The resulting impact

---

21. Ibid., lines 60–62.
22. Ibid., lines 90–91.
23. Sykes, *Hollow Men*, 27.

Happy Without the Meal

goes beyond the college classroom and campus. Sykes points out:

> Authority of all kinds—of the author, of history, of language, of reason—could now be attacked as "fascistic," "tyrannical," "imperialistic," and "hegemonic." If language is "duplicitous," as theorists like Jacques Derrida insisted, then it can be decoded and deconstructed to make whatever political point was desired.[24]

Postmodernism and deconstruction are certainly very challenging concepts to digest. But reasonable points can be seen in such a worldview. For instance life is in large part a mystery, with "ultimate truth" beyond the reach of any one person's works, thoughts, or writings. At the same time it is clear that postmodern thought is highly critical of modern concepts such as morality, virtues, and purpose in life. In place of these traditional values are the related philosophies of nihilism and relativism. Nihilism is a form of thinking that rejects meaning in life, while relativism rejects the notion that truths exists and can be known. These are not mere philosophical and academic terms that have no real impact upon society. Such ways of experiencing the world must necessarily encourage anxiety, apathy, and unhappiness.

The recognition of this imbalance in higher education is becoming increasingly recognized. Many universities have gone down a slippery slope where the historical mission of helping to form the good person has been lost. In his gutsy book *Excellence Without a Soul*, thirty-year Harvard professor and eight-year Harvard College dean

---

24. Ibid.

The Nature of Things

Harry Lewis relays how Harvard and many universities have lost sight of their educational mission in a consumptive culture.

> Over the decades I have heard many academic discussions about teaching, about the curriculum, about grading, about athletics, and about responding to student misdeeds. I have almost never heard discussions among professors about making students better people. Professors are warned to look for signs of emotional distress in students and to steer them to mental health services. But what most students need more then psychiatric referrals is help shaping the lives that they themselves, and not their parents, will lead. Presidents, deans, and professors rarely tell students simple truths.[25]

Lewis provides a historical account of how Harvard has regressed from its original "grand mission . . . to create knowledge, educate youth, and to teach what young people should know and how they should live" toward an emphasis on international study and world experience.[26] The only objective truth remaining at Harvard might now be the *Veritas* on the school's crest. Lewis cautions that such an elitist and relativistic approach is out of step with our nation's morals and character. He adds that America's elite colleges are still valued, but that the general public is growing increasingly skeptical of them because they increasingly fail to teach or uphold virtuous standards.

Lewis tells an insightful story that exemplifies the impact a culture of consumerism and relativism has on a campus.

25. H. Lewis, *Excellence Without a Soul*, xv.
26. Ibid., 25.

Happy Without the Meal

> In the saddest cases, parents trying to obtain advantages instead cripple their children's development of personal agency. A student who turned in a plagiarized paper provided as an excuse a novel variation on the old "I turned in my notes by mistake" argument. He suffered, he said, from a disabling inability to write. The student's typist must have typed up his notes rather than his actual paper, and he turned in what the typist gave him without checking it. The typist, known only by her first name, had disappeared from the face of the earth. The processes meant to accommodate this young man's disability had instead victimized him. His family assured us that they would take the College to court for failing to accommodate his disability if he were found guilty of plagiarism. It was not his fault that the paper the professor received, delivered by the student's own hand and with the student's name on it, was the work of others.[27]

Lewis is painfully honest in his concern for the decline of integrity at Harvard, confessing:

> The university has lost, indeed has willingly surrendered, its moral authority to shape the souls of its students. Harvard wants its students to be safe and healthy, but security and therapy are the limits of its ambition. Harvard articulates no ideals of what it means to be a good person, as opposed to a well person.[28]

In the summer of 2011, at my own university, we had a faculty development series of discussions regarding better ways to engage students and faculty in the learn-

27. Ibid., 157.
28. Ibid., 160.

The Nature of Things

ing process. A wonderfully insightful book, *The Heart of Higher Education: A Call to Renewal* by Parker Palmer and Arthur Zajonc, was used to guide this work. The authors lay out an eloquent discussion on the devolution of universities into "discipline silos," where walls separate knowledge into distinct departments. Courses are taught in fields such as psychology, sociology, history, and political science in a fragmented manner, almost as if there were no overlap between these disciplines.

The walling off of student and subject into isolated compartments has been a direct result of postmodern thinking. The authors sum up the negative impact of such ideology on campus culture:

> Too often, in the wake of postmodern deconstruction, a radical pluralistic confusion and an oddly playful nihilism are all that remains. The important insights concerning the social construction and content of texts are swamped by an iconoclastic zeal that slays meaning whenever it arises.[29]

These words are beautifully written and at the same time striking: "an oddly playful nihilism" and a "zeal that slays meaning whenever it arises." I've read them many times. They resonate strongly in me. While certainly accurate, they ought to belong in a teen vampire novel rather than a book on higher education. Zajonc draws upon his decades of teaching and how postmodern thought plays out in the classroom:

> Since the 1980s, I have sat across from some of Amherst College's brightest students who, having mastered the philosophy and techniques of

29. Palmer and Zajonc, *Heart of Higher Education*, 63.

> deconstruction advocated by Derrida, Foucault, and Lacan, lamented the subsequent loss of meaning and sought ways to regain the value of the text themselves and a purpose to their lives.[30]

Whether or not students have come across such writers, I too sense a growing frustration when they perceive that learning is devoid of meaning. When teaching our Introduction to Sociology course I use a text that relays a 240-year historical incident that resonates strongly with the challenges faced today in higher education in particular, and in our broader culture in general. In 1774 Virginia commissioners offered to provide a proper schooling to young Iroquois Indian boys at the college of William and Mary, where they would be cared for and educated like the Colonialists. The Iroquois, out of politeness took a day to consider the offer and then responded:

> We know that you highly esteem the kind of learning taught in colleges, and that the maintenance of our young men, while with you, would be very expensive to you. We're convinced, therefore, that you mean to do us good by your proposal, and we thank you heartily. But you, who are wise, must know that different nations have different conceptions of things; and you will not, therefore, take it amiss if our ideas of this kind of education happens not to be the same with yours.
>
> We have had some experience of it. Several of our young people were formerly brought up in the colleges of the northern province. They were instructed in all your sciences. But when they came back to us, they were bad runners, ignorant of every means of living in the woods,

30. Ibid.

The Nature of Things

unable to bear either cold or hunger, knew neither how to build a cabin, take a deer, or kill an enemy, spoke our language imperfectly, and therefore were neither fit for hunters, warriors, nor councilors. They were totally good for nothing.

We are, however, not the less obliged for your kind offer, though we decline accepting. To show our grateful sense of it, if the gentlemen of Virginia shall send us a dozen of their sons, we would take great care in their education, instruct them in all we know, and make men of them.[31]

Is Everything Just Relative?

A key theme that emerges from the Iroquois story is not anti education, but a positive belief in person's or peoples' inherent ability to discern purpose and meaning. Both what is of value and what is not. Postmodern thinking has made its way into popular culture, driving home the belief that living a happy life is not possible without some expert knowledge, product, or service. It's as if the "average" person simply isn't smart enough or educated enough to know how to live.

Certainly what is true is many-sided. If two people come upon the scene of an auto accident, one from the north and the other from the south, they will each have a different view of the scene. But relativism goes beyond perspective, arguing that there is no absolute truth, let alone "right" thing to do. A person's belief is their reality. In this case helping is an individual choice, as there is no right or wrong in any situation.

---

31. Carroll, "Indians of the Six Nations," 240.

Happy Without the Meal

Relativism is marked by a kind of crass sophistication, a misguided confidence in our collective scientific minds. This is certainly not new. In an interview given to the *Saturday Evening Post* in 1929, Albert Einstein himself disputed what the popularized idea of relativity had become:

> The meaning of relativity has been widely misunderstood. Philosophers play with the word like a child with a doll. Relativity, as I see it, merely denotes that certain physical and mechanical facts, which have been regarded as positive and permanent, are relative with regard to certain other facts in the sphere of physics and mechanics. It does not mean that everything in life is relative and that we have the right to turn the whole world mischievously topsy-turvy.[32]

In spite of Einstein's prophetic warning, our culture has indeed turned topsy-turvy. One of the most profound ways this has occurred is in our understanding of what it means to be happy. Our marketing culture has been able to remake happiness because of the wider cultural shift toward relativism. Similar to postmodern thinking, relativism can be understood as individually created truth. Good and bad, right and wrong doesn't exist objectively. They are subjective, to be decided by the individual. Opinion now equals fact.

Relativism is bolstered by our twenty-four/seven media where entertainment now morphs with news coverage. Fifty years ago daily newspapers provided news reports and three major networks highlighted the most important daily events during an hour-long evening

32. Viereck, "What Life Means," lines 43–51.

The Nature of Things

broadcast. Today literally thousands of network, cable, radio, and Internet programs provide immediate news coverage and commentary tailored primarily to targeted audiences. Add to those the seeming endless political and popular commentaries, there now are experts on every imaginable subject area. We can now shop for "factual information" to fit our desired worldview. To put it another way, we can easily create our own truth.

Daily saturation from the countless news and entertainment outlets leads to chronic cultural anxiety. Almost simultaneously we hear both of the latest tragedies along with products promising happiness. These two opposing forces are presented in the extreme. The incredible information technology has the negative side effect of false superiority. Not only do we have instant global updates, but we also have supposed control of our personal world through our choice of music downloads, texting, fast food, and any material goods. At the same time we keep turning to the latest diet, self-help book, and fashion and health magazines because "experts" have authored them. We're frightened by gloom and doom reports, then seek shelter in ease and expert advice.

There is no place in society for suffering, aging, and certainly not death. Commercials tell us to fear wrinkles, and to fear hair loss and thin eyelashes, now a medical condition known as "hypotrichosis." Our culture of consumption makes an ally of fear and masks the reality of the human condition. An inevitable part of that condition is that humans are mortal. Our physical bodies will die. That seldom-discussed part of life has such huge implications because our view about life after death dictates how we live each day.

Three

The Rise and Fall of Health and Habits

You can't live on amusement.
It is the froth on water—an inch deep
and then the mud.
—George MacDonald (1824–1905)

Highlights in the History of Health and Illness

The modern history of disease can be traced back to the Middle Ages, around AD 800 to 1300. Recovering from the desolation of the Dark Ages, people again were able to establish a sense of community. As folks gathered, towns emerged and cities began to swell. However with this progress also came the difficulty of communicable diseases such as leprosy and smallpox, primarily due to poor sanitation and lack of advanced medical knowledge.

Infections passed quickly and often led to epidemics and pandemics. Between 1347 and 1351 the bubonic

The Rise and Fall of Health and Habits

plague, or "black death" ravaged upwards of 50 percent of Europe's population. Without practical medical information well-intentioned interventions oftentimes did more harm than good. Thinking illness was caused by poisoned body fluids, a sore throat would be treated by cutting into a vein and draining blood. Such practices continued even through colonial times. George Washington died prematurely because he was bled profusely in the attempt to treat pneumonia and a severe sore throat he had caught after inspecting Mount Vernon on horseback in stormy weather.

It wasn't until only four hundred years ago, in the early 1700s, that life expectancy began to increase. However this increase was not primarily due to improved medications or health care as commonly believed, but to several key social changes. Warfare tactics evolved, moving battles and soldiers away from cities, lessening both the horrible impact of combat upon civilians and the spread of infection. Improved agricultural practices and access to new lands allowed for improved crop harvests. This improved access to food and nutrition made for heartier physical constitutions, helping people fight off disease and infection. With improved living conditions women were able to spend less time engaging in physically draining fieldwork, enabling them to spend more time nurturing their children. In addition, women began having fewer children at an older age, improving survival rates for both mother and child.[1]

If we were to contrast the past hundred years to any other period in history, there would be no comparison as

---

1. Weitz, "Social Sources," 21.

to the immense ease and comfort that is now available to most people. The same holds true for longevity. Between 1900 and 1930 alone life expectancy in the United States rose by an average of ten years, from to forty-nine to fifty-nine. Thirty years later, in 1960, life expectancy increased by another eleven years to seventy years of age.[2] Average life expectancy is now approaching eighty years of age.

It is important to recognize that it is only during the past hundred years, just a few generations ago, that people in Western societies have lived long enough to die primarily of diseases related to age. Throughout nearly all of human history, most people died at a much younger age, primarily from infections and parasitic diseases. By the early 1900s, on average people began living long enough to die of old age.

This shift from a society confronted by communicable and parasitic diseases that result in low life expectancy to a society where people have the benefit of high life expectancy but with deteriorating and long-lasting disease is known as the "epidemiological transition." In the United States this shift occurred during the early 1900s, only one hundred years ago. During this past century we have experienced massive gains in medicine, science, and technology, which have led to the quality of life we now experience. The common assumption is that the epidemiological transition occurred because of improved medicines, vaccinations, and surgical procedures. However that's not the case. The primary cause enabling us to live a full life and die of "old age" is improved sanitation, nutrition, and living conditions.

2. Shrestha, "Life Expectancy," table 1.

Medicine or Magic?

For some time now researchers have been shedding light on the limits of medicine, becoming aware that overreliance upon surgery and drugs could lead to disastrous individual and social consequences. A classic example is the work of researcher and physician Thomas McKeown (1912–1988). In his book *The Role of Medicine: Dream, Mirage, or Nemesis*, McKeown looks at the history of health and illness, with a focus on the development of medicine in England since the 1900s. His evidence strongly suggests that clinical interventions, while invaluable, are not nearly as influential to declining mortality as other factors, such as diet, environment, and behaviors.

In the preface to the second edition of his book he touches on the flak he received when publishing his initial findings. Critics "interpreted the book as an attack on clinical medicine." However McKeown goes to great length not to attack medicine, but to make the case that while medical advances have been remarkable, they've also had a mesmerizing impact in culture. He writes, "the conclusion that medical intervention is often less effective than has been thought in no way diminishes the significance of their clinical function."[3]

Scholars John McKinlay and Sonja McKinlay built on this research in the United States and also emphasize the difficulty calling into question the invincibility associated with science and medicine. Thirty years ago the authors pointed out:

---

3. McKeown, *Role of Medicine*, vii.

Happy Without the Meal

> The modern "heresy" that medical care (as it is traditionally conceived) is generally unrelated to improvement in the health of populations (as distinct from individuals) is still dismissed as unthinkable in much the same way as the so-called heresies of former times. And this despite a long history of support in popular and scientific writings as well as from able minds in a variety of disciplines.[4]

Drawing upon mortality rates adjusted for age and sex in America from 1900 until 1973, they came to similar findings as McKeown and conclude that medical interventions:

> appear to have contributed little to the overall decline in mortality in the United States since about 1900. . . . it is estimated that at most 3.5 percent of the total decline in mortality since 1900 could be ascribed to medical measures introduced for the diseases considered here.[5]

Other research points to a slightly more generous figure, suggesting that enhanced medical treatments account for a gain of approximately seven years in life expectancy over the past century.[6]

Scholar Rose Weitz contrasts the dramatic shift in diseases during the past hundred years, making the distinction that the main cause of death has moved from infection in 1900 to chronic conditions a century later. She points out that "the top killers in 1900—influenza, pneumonia, and tuberculosis—were infectious diseases,

4. J. McKinlay and S. McKinlay, "Questionable Contribution," 405.

5. Ibid., 425.

6. Bunker et al., "Improving Health," 238.

the top killers currently—heart disease and cancer—are chronic diseases primarily associated with middle-aged and older populations. These diseases now far outpace infectious diseases as causes of death."[7]

Historically speaking this is very good news! We are living longer lives than at any other time in history. During the past one hundred years our life expectancy has increased by approximately thirty years, a full one-third of a lifetime. Yet even with such remarkable gains in improved health, material goods, and medical advancements in the very recent past, our society seems *less* rather than *more* grateful for our good fortune. People seem hungrier and less satisfied than ever. Looking back on history, we could have reasonably guessed that with such abundance, mankind would have advanced. Having more time and resources on our hands should have led us to a higher cultural, physical, psychological, and spiritual plane. But the very opposite seems to have happened.

> Our body has this defect that, the more it is provided care and comforts, the more needs and desires it finds.
>
> —St. Teresa of Avila (1515–1582)

Medicine has made advances through the use of what is called the "medical model." The medical model refers to the traditional way doctors diagnose and treat illness in Western cultures since the development of the scientific method. Diagnosis of a problem is accomplished by gathering information from the patient's medical history,

---

7. Weitz, "Social Sources," 28.

current symptoms, and any number of analytic tests. The diagnosis drives the treatment, or established method for curing an illness.

While the benefits of this model are vast, they are limited to the physical, biological aspects of human beings. The medical model takes an objective, one-dimensional view of humanity. While oftentimes quite helpful, the model sees people only as mechanical entities, not unlike the way an auto mechanic would view a car.

The medical model has been astoundingly effective in curing or relieving physical disease and sickness from a range of biological problems. From taking aspirin for a minor headache to vaccinations that have virtually conquered polio and chicken pox to heart-replacement surgery that gives patients a new lease on life, medical advancements have been miracle-like in their helpfulness. Largely because of such success this model has also seeped in the cultural perception of health and illness. We now commonly assume that almost any condition can be countered with some type of modern medicine, with at times no attention being given to a holistic view of the person. A more holistic perspective (often termed "biopsychosocial") recognizes the physical makeup of the person, but also sees the emotional, mental, social, and spiritual nature as well.

The strict application of the medical model of health and illness has for some time now been criticized for neglecting the many dimensions that make up a person, influencing his or her health. Doctors have been working to help people feel better, but sense that much more is going on behind the scenes that impacts wellness. Medical sociologist John McKinlay shares a simple, but telling parable that conveys this experience:

> Sometimes it feels like this. There I am standing by the shore of a swiftly flowing river and I hear the cry of a drowning man. So I jump into the river, put my arms around him, pull him to shore and apply artificial respiration. Just when he begins to breathe, there is another cry for help. So I jump into the river, reach him, pull him to shore, apply artificial respiration, and then just as he begins to breathe, another cry for help. So back in the river again, reaching, pulling, applying, breathing, and then another yell. Again and again, without end, goes the sequence. You know, I am so busy jumping in, pulling them to shore, applying artificial respiration, that I have *no* time to see who the hell is upstream pushing them all in.[8]

Some good lessons can be learned from this tale. Society seems to be obsessed on the immediate, here and now of health. We tend to have a quick fix mentality. We want to have our cake and eat it too . . . literally. Our reasoning goes something like this. We pull up to a drive-through and buy a value meal, but are sure to order the diet soda to keep the nutrition balanced. When excess weight is put on we go to see the doctor who prescribes medication for high blood pressure, type 2 diabetes, and depression. Lost in plain sight is the actual cause of extra body weight: eating more calories than we burn off. Or as McKinlay writes, "We should somehow cease our preoccupation with this short-term, problem-specific tinkering

---

8. J. McKinlay, "Case for Refocusing," 502–3.

and begin focusing our attention upstream, where the real problems lie."[9]

Making our way upstream, what do we find? Towering over us is nothing less than the glacial headwaters of products and services promising to satisfy our every thirst. These are the food, entertainment, tobacco, alcohol, and social media industries, to list but a few. McKinlay would coin the phrase "manufacturers of illness" to describe "those individuals, interest groups, and organizations which, in addition to producing material goods and services, also produce, as an inevitable by-product, widespread morbidity and mortality."[10] McKinlay shared this classic analogy of people being pushed (oftentimes willingly) into the water forty years ago. He was primarily concerned with the overconsumption of food and drink, addictions to cigarettes and drugs, unsafe driving habits, and the pollution of our planet. As an example he cites statistics for food overconsumption, and points out that 40 percent of Americans are overweight or obese at the time of his writings. Here we are now forty years later and that figure has nearly *doubled*, reaching a whopping 70 percent.[11]

McKinlay's work was prophetic. Not only have our waistlines expanded, but by an even greater degree so has the availability of consumables. In thinking about consumption it's important to pause and tease out key subtleties in the phrase *manufacturers of illness*. The production and availability of goods and services is in most cases in-

9. Ibid., 503.
10. Ibid.
11. Fryar et al., "Prevalence of Overweight," line 2.

nocuous, neither good nor bad. Products and amenities are typically, at their core, inoffensive. A hamburger, cell phone, aspirin, cold beer, pair of sneakers, car, or whatever, has a function, a use. Living in a free society we can choose to use them or not.

But what has occurred gradually during this past century at an ever increasing rate is what McKinlay refers as the "inevitable by-product, widespread morbidity and mortality" due to overconsumption.[12] Morbidity refers to being unwell in some physical, emotional, mental, or spiritual sense, which mortality refers to as bodily death. The more people consume just to consume, the less well they become. Again, going back to natural principles, human beings are not cyborgs, or virtual beings. We're not designed to continually ingest. When this occurs our system will experience overload and begin to break down in some manner.

When Progress Leads to Discontentment

And the effect of overconsumption has been widespread. Research now shows that American's today are likely to suffer mental and emotional problems at a higher rate than those who lived in the past several decades. Certain forms of research use a technique known as "meta-analyses," which essentially means examining the findings of a host of other separate studies that have looked at a topic area. One such study was conducted in 2010 and published in the journal *Clinical Psychology Review*. The study examined the differences in psychopathology (the

12. J. McKinlay, "Case for Refocusing," 503.

study of mental distress or illness) among high school and college students in 2007 compared to those in 1938.

This historical analysis shows that culture does impact the health of individuals. The authors found that one of the key changes during the past century has been a movement away from intrinsic goals toward extrinsic goals in our society. Young adults from a few generations ago embraced the idea that life was about meaning, purpose, and people. They were energized by a cause beyond their own self-interests, whether faith, family, community, or country. Putting self second was not a heroic virtue at the time, but a common value. This is one of the reasons why those who lived through the Great Depression and served at home and abroad through World War II have been called the "greatest generation."

With the advent of material abundance has come cultural messaging that morphs product with person. Instead of using goods simply to satisfy a need, people have begun to identify with the brand or meaning attached to the product itself. It's sort of an attempt to live vicariously through merchandise. Such efforts fail to provide any real, lasting satisfaction. The researchers found that:

> People pursuing extrinsic goals such as money, looks, and status are more likely to be anxious and depressed. A focus on extrinsic goals undermines the satisfaction of the important intrinsic goals of competence, affiliation, and autonomy and leads to poor relationships and antisocial behaviors.[13]

---

13. Twenge et al., "Birth Cohort Increases," 146.

The Rise and Fall of Health and Habits

Evidence from this meta-analysis supports these ideas. High school and college students have experienced steadily increasing rates of emotional distress from the 1930s until the present. Researchers found that in 1938 up to 5 percent of college students experienced clinical symptoms of mental illness. By 2007 that rate grew to a remarkable 25 percent, or one-quarter of students scoring above standard cutoff scores suggesting some form of emotional distress. The researchers state that a culture of consumption has harmed mental health:

> As American culture has increasingly valued extrinsic and self-centered goals such as money and status, while increasingly devaluing community, affiliation, and finding meaning in life, the mental health of American youth has suffered. . . . materialism, individualism, and impossibly high expectations have led to an epidemic of poor mental health in the U.S. and other Western nations.[14]

These findings are even more remarkable when we reflect upon the standard of living and world events in the 1930s compared with contemporary society. The Great Depression was one of the most difficult times in American history, lasting approximately twelve years from the stock market collapse of 1929 until factories began hiring as the United States prepared to enter World War II in 1941. Unemployment reached its peak in 1933 with a quarter of the population having no jobs. In that same year eleven thousand out of twenty-five thousand banks had failed. The FDIC had not yet been established, so bank failure meant people lost their life savings in an

14. Ibid., 153.

Happy Without the Meal

instant. This was the experience of my own family. My dad told me the story of his heart breaking when as a young boy he watched his mom break down crying because her life savings vanished.

In addition to economic collapse, farmers battled to survive the Dust Bowl during the early to mid-1930s where drought scorched over a million acres of farmland, forcing thousands to move from rural lands to towns and cities. Here many relied upon soup kitchens or breadlines to survive. These were often run by churches and private charities. Shantytowns popped up throughout the land where homeless individuals and families would cobble together crude dwellings from anything they could find, such as scraps of metal, wood, canvas, or abandoned cars.

While factory work brought initial economic relief in the early 1940s, World War II was a tremendously difficult time at home and abroad. Nearly 300,000 military service members died in action, and another 670,000 were wounded. Untold numbers have dealt with the psychological horrors of battle. Life at home was demanding as well. The Japanese attack on Pearl Harbor in 1941 instantly altered daily life as panic gripped the nation. If a military assault on Hawaii could be successful why not others along the Pacific coast or even inland? Necessities such as food, clothing, and gasoline were rationed. The government issued ration stamps so that people could only buy their share of basic products such as produce, meat, sugar, butter, coffee, shoes, tires, and fuel oil.

It is now common to carry a personal cell phone, stop in for a quick super-sized meal or snack at any of the dozens of fast food chains, and download music to an iPod or similar digital device. Not only are these activities now ordinary, but many also consider them to be essentials. Not having a cell phone creates anxiety. Going one day without checking social media status updates is intolerable. Much of what our culture dictates as "essential" *did not even exist* fifty years ago. Looking at our day-to-day lives (food, drinks, conveniences, education, entertainment, travel, communications, social media, etc.), Americans with average household incomes, those earning roughly $60,000 per year, experience a standard of living at approximately the *top 5 percent wealthiest of the 1940s*.[15]

Drawing a contrast between society today and life back in the 1930s and 1940s based on cultural conditions and material progress, one would reasonably assume that people are much happier now, or at least should be. Yet research tells us that just the opposite seems to be occurring. Several overlapping changes have occurred which help explain the paradox. The concept of *manufacturers of illness* as described by McKinlay in the 1970s still applies. However since that time marketing strategies have become increasingly aggressive to capture our attention and brand loyalty. A key shift occurred only in the past few decades that spurred this on.

> Advertising treats all products with the reverence and the seriousness due to sacraments.[16]
>
> —Thomas Merton (1915–1968)

---

15. Scott and Leonhardt, "Shadowy Lines," lines 230–32.
16. Merton, *Conjectures*, 232.

Happy Without the Meal

During the 1990s manufacturers reached a point where they could no longer market their products primarily based on utility or plain usefulness. Markets had become saturated in Western societies. There was and continues to be an overabundance of goods and services. Consumers not only have virtually endless choices of basic items such as food, drink, and clothing, we also have enormous selections of what would formerly have been considered luxury items, such as high-end vehicles, designer cloths, social media, apps, and gaming devices.

Because of such market saturation, corporations have had to be much more creative in order to sell their goods. Advertisers realized that they must shift toward selling "beliefs" rather than mere products. A new and fantastically effective tactic was developed and deployed: "emotional branding." Simply put, the goal of emotional branding is to have customers develop an intimate, loyal, even spiritual relationship, not only with a product, but also with the image attached to that product. To have the folks feel that they are distinctive and belong to the messaging associated with the product by being stamped, or "branded."

In the article "Branded for Life," Tom Sine warns:

> The world is beginning to look like an American strip mall, complete with KFC, Pizza Hut, and the Golden Arches . . . The destination of McWorld's economic engineering is a global shopping mall where our identity, our common humanity, and even our spirituality are derived from our consumerism . . . We have moved into a new neighborhood. We are not simply dealing with the issues of consumerism that we contended with in the '70s and '80s. In the 21st

The Rise and Fall of Health and Habits

century, global marketers have taken an entirely new focus that is much more seductive than anything we have seen before.[17]

In a free market society there is certainly nothing wrong with companies wanting to promote products, develop an attractive image, and make profits. The challenge comes into play when the message suggests that ultimate meaning and happiness can be reached through consumption. From a corporate perspective, this approach is necessary. Because of market saturation advertisers simply must create a need for products. The message to consumers is that fulfillment—physical, emotional, and spiritual—can be found through continual experience of fun and pleasure.

The perhaps unfortunate truth is that this *can't* happen. As humans we experience life with certain limitations behaviorally just as we do physically. Psychologists have coined this important emotional limitation as "hedonic adaptation." This dry-sounding phrase disguises a very interesting behavioral principle. The root of the word "hedonic" is from the Greek *hedone*, which means "pleasure." Adaptation refers to adapting or adjusting to an environment.

As humans we have been hardwired to experience a wide range of emotions in response to life's circumstances. However, the lows and highs we experience from good times and bad tend to last temporarily, and then recede back to our normal state or level of happiness. This is a critically important defense mechanism, because as mortals we all have the universal experience of suffering in

17. Sine, "Branded for Life," lines 55–56, 89–90, 106–8.

Happy Without the Meal

some manner. The problems of life come in many forms, whether mental, physical, or spiritual. If the deep pain experienced by the death of a loved one, divorce, crisis of faith, physical injury, or illness were to persist without relief, daily life would become unbearable.

However the pendulum swings in both directions. The same principle holds true for pleasurable experiences. While we may not want to let go of the high, we can't help but to adjust to the fun, to "level off" from the initial high. The new car no longer feels "new," after only a few months. The exciting cell phone upgrade begins to dull within weeks. The "happy" in the Happy Meal dissipates within hours if not minutes.

> Everything in excess is opposed to nature.
> —HIPPOCRATES (460–370 BC)

When teaching this principle to my students I use the abbreviation "HA" to remember hedonic adaptation because as far as consumption leading to happiness, the joke is on us! In fact psychologists use the more visual phrase "hedonic treadmill" to describe this same reality. Just as running on a treadmill won't get you anywhere, getting more "stuff" doesn't lead to contentment.

The principle of hedonic adaptation was identified by psychologists in the 1970s, but writers have recognized this same principle for quite some time. Fulton Sheen in his 1949 book *Peace of Soul* observed:

> Uncontrolled desires grow like weeds and stifle the spirit. Material possessions bring a relative pleasure for a time, but sooner or later a malaise

is experienced; a sense of emptiness, a feeling
that something is wrong comes over the soul.[18]

Of the several courses I teach on a regular basis, by far the one that fills most quickly and is most popular among my students is Sociology 320, Social Psychology of Addictions. The course is essentially split into two sections. The first part specifically explores habitual use of alcohol and other drugs, while the second looks at "other addictions." These are primarily behavioral compulsions, such as Internet, texting, gaming, social media, and shopping addictions. Having taught this course for over five years, several interesting themes have emerged.

First, students seem to be drawn to the course even before learning what that term means, because they sense they're living in a culture of addiction. This phrase refers to "an informal social network in which group norms (ways of perceiving, thinking, feeling, and behaving) promote excessive drug use."[19] As we move through the course we progress beyond "group norms" and "drug use" and apply this concept to our culture of consumption. When initially teaching the course I had the impression that it would be difficult for students to look behind the marketing veil, so to speak, since they've grown up being saturated by marketing. Happily that's not been the case. Time and again when we near the end of the course most students are able to easily see how corporations profit from a compulsive culture. It's so much fun to teach this course and see these unpretentious learners laugh at the

---

18. Sheen, *Peace of Soul*, 27.
19. White, *Pathways from the Culture*, 5.

realization that yes, many times they've been duped by an incredibly effective marketing industry.

Second, many of these students show tremendous courage and a thirst for what is true. As part of the course requirements students have an option of writing a modest term paper or taking part in a forty-day abstinence exercise where they choose something they enjoy doing on a daily basis and give that thing up for just under six weeks. They then write a paper of personal reflection and give a presentation to the class based upon that experience. Students have selected a wide range of activities from which to abstain, including favorite foods and drinks, cigarettes, shopping, and nail biting. However the most common activity by far has been some form of social media, such as gaming, surfing the Internet, staying connected via Facebook, or texting.

Although the term paper is the less difficult option, the vast majority select the more demanding abstinence activity. And while it is true that a small percentage of students will put minimal effort into the project, most not only engage but are genuinely excited at the challenge. They learn rather quickly how easily we can become overly attached to something and the subsequent feeling of being stressed much of the time. During their presentations I commonly hear them literally laugh in comic relief at the freeing awareness that they've been devoted to something they actually care very little about.

A third theme that has emerged from the course is an outgrowth of the second, namely the profound influence that technology has on our psyche. When unchecked it can be as addictive and damaging as any drug. Given that it is only fifteen weeks in length and is an undergraduate course, I stress the importance of not stamping their chosen behaviors as "addictive" but instead "attached" as they are not clinicians and I don't want them labeling themselves. At the same time, many are fascinated to discover how virtual much of their lives have become. They report that the more virtual they become the more tired and old they feel. My sense of their experience is that they are relieved to know they've been battling phantoms, and that there is another way. They don't have to be tired at twenty.

Techno-Babble and the Instant Gratification Myth

Along with the magnificent advances in technology has come a dangerous pitfall. We are tempted, most times subconsciously, to equate product development with personal growth. Clicking the "okay" button to send a text instantly somehow equates with who we are as a person, our worth, and abilities. Having the latest app on our smartphone makes us smart. With 1,500 Facebook friends we'll never be lonely again. Recognition of believing such falsehoods is not new. Over fifty years ago Trappist monk and writer Thomas Merton saw this on the horizon:

> The real root-sin of modern man is that, in ignoring and contemning *being*, and especially his own being, he has made his *existence* a disease and an affliction. And, strangely, he has done this with all kinds of vitalistic excuses, proclaiming at every turn that he stands on frontiers of new abundance and permanent bliss. This ambiguity and arbitrariness appear most clearly in

> technology. There is nothing wrong with technology in itself. It could indeed serve to deepen and perfect the quality of men's existence and in some ways it *has* done this. As Lewis Mumford said: "Too many thought not only that mechanical progress would be a positive aid to human improvement, which is true, *but that mechanical progress is the equivalent of human improvement,* which turns out to be sheer non-sense." We have not even begun to plumb the depths of nonsense into which this absurd error has plunged us.[20]

Fortunately, as far as social media is concerned, we have begun to plumb the depths of nonsense. Numerous research studies have revealed the irony that overuse of devices that promise to bring us closer to others have just the opposite effect. They tend to increase loneliness, anxiety, and dependence. Spending too much time on the Internet has been correlated with insomnia, social dysfunction, depression, and anxiety. Cell phone overuse is related to poor sleep patterns, emotional dependence, thinking errors such as "I can't live without my cell phone," and anxiety.

One of these studies was conducted in 2010 at the University of Maryland, where two hundred students did without all social media for twenty-four hours. At the end of this brief time period they reported on a designated website whether they were successful or not and gave their reflections on abstaining. The findings in this study were startling. Students used the same verbiage of substance abuse to describe their addiction to social media, such as "I clearly am addicted and the dependency

20. Merton, *Conjectures*, 222.

The Rise and Fall of Health and Habits

is sickening," and "I feel like most people these days are in a similar situation, for between having a Blackberry, a laptop, a television, and an iPod, people have become unable to shed their media skin." The researchers report that "most college students are not just unwilling, but functionally unable to be without their media links to the world."[21]

These technologies are addictive because overuse triggers what is known as a dopamine induced loop (DIL). Dopamine is an adrenergic stimulator, a chemical that is released in our brain to makes us alert and ready for action. When dopamine is released we experience an increased heart rate, higher blood pressure, and a sense that everything is moving faster. Cell phone, gaming, and social media advertisers sell the message that their products will satisfy our need for fun and excitement. Because of the three phases of the DIL we know they can't.

We'll use a brief cell phone texting sequence as a simple example. In the first stage of the DIL a person feels a "hit" of dopamine that is released in the brain. When we send or receive a text it is typically a pleasurable experience. This leads to the second stage where we need more "hits" to get that same brief high, so we begin to overuse because we aren't satisfied. This helps to explain why social networking tools often lead to anxiety. We become used to our gadgets and yearn for more positive feedback, then feel down when the messages stop. The final stage takes us back to the "HA" behavioral principle of hedonic adaptation, whereby we quickly become used to changes in life, both positive and negative, and adjust to our "normal" level of happiness.

21. Moeller et al., "Day Without Media," 6–11.

Happy Without the Meal

Scholarly research on this topic has filtered down into popular news coverage. The July 16, 2012 cover of *Newsweek* leads with the title, "iCRAZY; Panic. Depression. Psychosis: How Connection Addiction is Rewiring Our Brains." Beneath this title is an image of a young girl holding her hands to her ears and screaming. In the lead article Tony Dokoupil reviews the new but expanding research that is showing how media overuse is having a host of harmful effects on our culture in general and youth in particular. The two themes that run through his article are that these devices are addictive, and that those who overuse them become exhausted. More troubling is the response to this new form of emotional distress. Instead of lessening the use or just shutting off these devices, many turn to medication.

> Overwhelmed by the velocity of their lives, we turn to prescription drugs, which helps explain why America runs on Xanax (and why rehab admissions for benzodiazepines, the ingredient in Xanax and other anti-anxiety drugs, have tripled since the late 1990s).[22]

To paraphrase a corny old Johnny Lee country western song, our culture seems to be *"lookin' for love in all the wrong places."*

---

22. Dokoupil, "Is the Onslaught?," 30.

Four

The Manufacturing of Illness

> One of the ironies of our culture is that no matter how much health is improved (as evidenced by decreased mortality rates, increased life expectancy, and improved health care), the reporting of health problems continues to rise.[1]
> —PETER CONRAD (1945–)

The idea that some*thing* will make us happy has seeped deeply into society during the past several decades. Perhaps nowhere more troubling has this taken root than in our understanding of health itself. As our culture has grown increasingly secular, there has been a rising focus on the material, the physical. Just as manufacturers promise nothing but bliss, the health industry has increasingly followed suit by developing products promising relief from any conceivable discomfort.

---

1. Conrad, *Medicalization of Society*, 149.

Happy Without the Meal

It is of course completely natural to desire good health and to want to avoid illness. However, living in a free market society we are reminded to be aware that the health care industry functions much like most other industry . . . for profit. The more diagnosable illnesses that exist, the more products can be developed to treat ailments. And we seem to be finding new illnesses almost every day.

When teaching the course Sociology of Health, I begin with two activities. First, I pass out a short list of "medical conditions" and ask students to give their opinion whether these are issues requiring a doctor's attention or not. Included in the list are disorders such as diabetes, bone fracture, cancer, and pneumonia. I also add "thin eyelashes." When the responses are collected I ask the young learners why no one identified thin eyelashes as an illness. In general the response is that eyelashes are a rather small cosmetic issue, while the other conditions are more serious, with some being life threatening. I then share with the class that the medical term for thin eyelashes is "hypotrichosis," which refers to a less than normal amount of hair on the head or body. We then pull up a product website that promotes "Latisse" to treat this medical condition. I draw their attention to part of the site that reads, "Ask your doctor if Latisse is right for you."

Second, I ask my students if they can identify terms such as ADHD, ADD, Viagra, Botox, Prozac, Wellbutrin, and Zoloft. Within just a few minutes the class is able to describe these mental health diagnoses and medications. We then talk about how these now common disorders did not even exist thirty years ago. I point out in class that it is beyond the scope of the class (or of this book) to decide if these conditions are really medical issues or not. The purpose is to look at the cultural factors that have led to a dramatic shift where more and more people are being diagnosed, by professionals or themselves, with illnesses.

A central reason for this shift can be summed up by the term "medicalization." Medicalization is the process by which nonmedical problems become defined and treated as medical problems, usually in terms of illness or disorders. The term is actually not new, as sociologist, historians, bioethicists, psychologists, and physicians have written extensively about this for several decades. Most converge on the point that a cultural transformation is occurring where everyday life is being experienced as a pathology, or illness.

In his book *The Medicalization of Society: On Transformation of Human Conditions into Treatable Disorders*, Peter Conrad details this cultural shift:

> Behaviors that were once defined as immoral, sinful or criminal have been given medical meaning, moving them from badness to sickness. Certain common life processes have been medicalized as well, including anxiety and mood, menstruation, birth control, infertility, childbirth, menopause, aging, and death.[2]

Conrad explains that numerous social factors have influenced the rise of medicalization. Among these he lists the lessening role of religion in people's lives and the increasing belief that technology and products will solve problems. Our society has a cultural fixation on material progress. New and more must be better than old and less.

2. Ibid., 6.

Happy Without the Meal

He stresses the point that medicalization is a collective social action and not "medical imperialism." While many in the profession play a key role, particularly the medical and pharmaceutical industries, the general public is often "downright eager" to reduce their problems to a label and a pill. This mentality is part of the postmodern mindset and consumer culture, or as Conrad writes, "To put it crudely, medicalization of all sorts of life's problems is now a common part of our professional, consumer, and market culture."[3]

The Impact of Medicalization

While books and articles written about medicalization are now numerous, a classic research study known as the "Rosenhan experiment" was published in 1973 and helped to shine a light on the limits of medical diagnoses. Psychologist David Rosenhan along with seven other people (three psychologists, and a pediatrician, psychiatrist, painter, and housewife) contacted hospitals and made appointments with the admissions office. Upon arrival all eight complained only of hearing voices that were vague in nature, something like "empty," "hollow," or a "thud." Other than creating this symptom and giving fake names and occupations, there were no other deceptions. When questioned about health, family, personal history, relationships, and likes and dislikes, all eight responded as they would in their normal lives.

All of these would-be patients were easily admitted to hospital psychiatric wards and immediately stopped

3. Ibid., 14.

The Manufacturing of Illness

pretending to hear voices. Rosenhan reported that the eight did experience some anxiety early on, as they were sure they'd readily be discovered as healthy and in turn embarrassed for trying to pull off such a stunt. But this was not to happen. The study was designed so that once admitted, these patients were to be their usual selves and gain release from the hospital by behaving normally and convincing the staff of the simple fact that they were well.

None of the eight were detected as fakes by anyone on staff and all were given a mental health label. One was tagged "manic-depressive psychosis" and the others as "schizophrenic." The earliest time any of the eight gained release was seven days and the longest was fifty-two days, almost two full months! All were released with a diagnosis of schizophrenia "in remission." After the results were published, staff at a teaching and research hospital protested that the findings were by chance and that no such thing could occur at their facility. Rosenhan agreed to conduct a similar experiment and challenged the staff at the hospital to find the imposters. During the ninety days of this second experiment, out of 193 new patients admitted, 41 were strongly suspected of being fake by at least one staff member (attendant, nurse, physician, psychologist), and 23 seen as suspect by at least one psychiatrist. The results for this second experiment were as striking as the first, since Rosenhan sent *no one* to the hospital.

Although forty years old, Rosenhan's study and lessons learned apply today. He highlights the power of labeling as well as the role beliefs play in medicine. Beliefs transcend biology.

Happy Without the Meal

> A psychiatric label has a life and an influence of its own . . . labels, conferred by mental health professionals, are as influential on the patient as they are on his relatives and friends, and it should not surprise anyone that the diagnosis act on all of them is a self-fulfilling prophecy. Eventually, the patient himself accepts the diagnosis, with all of its surplus meanings and expectations, and behaves accordingly.[4]

In the four decades since his writing, medical care has moved well beyond the walls of a hospital and now enters through our TV sets and computer screens. The explosive use of psychotropic medicine—drugs to treat mental illness—has been driven by direct-to-consumer advertising sponsored by the pharmaceutical industry. These companies, collectively known as "Big Pharma," employ some of the most savvy psychologists and marketers tasked to promote their products. Their advertisements and commercials are wildly successful. We're now buying more and pricier drugs, with the popular ones rising faster than ever.

This is good news for Big Pharma, whose profits are massive. Earnings from the top ten pharmaceutical companies on the Fortune 500 surpassed the combined total of the remaining 490 companies on the list. When criticized for making such exorbitant proceeds, Big Pharma's public relations spin is often that profits are reinvested and put right back into research for new medicine to bring people relief and cure illness. While these companies do put 14

---

4. Scheff, *Being Mentally Ill*, quoted in Rosenhan, "Being Sane," lines 106–9.

The Manufacturing of Illness

percent of their earnings into research, a whopping 50 percent is pumped into marketing.[5]

Medicalization is increasingly recognized in academic and popular writings. Often termed "disease mongering," this sad practice of creating illnesses for the purpose of profit is perhaps beginning to be seen for what it is. The *Internal Medicine Journal* published a 2008 article, "Disease Mongering: Expanding the Boundaries of Treatable Disease," which shed light on this sensitive issue. The authors point out that health care has always had both moral and scientific underpinnings. Ethics is an inherent part of medicine. However the proliferation of technology has become a two-edged sword that can work for good *or* ill.

Disease mongering occurs when legitimate problems with living are greatly magnified. "Expanding the reach of a disorder typically involves distorting the prevalence and/or severity of a condition, the redefinition of risk factors as diseases, the inflation of mild or self-limiting symptomatic states and the pathologizing of normal human variation."[6] A central problem in confronting this practice is that so many positive advances have been made through science that it is difficult to distinguish the genuine from snake oil.

> The disease-mongering story is incomplete without accounting for contemporary medicine's profound dependence on technologies; the propensity of professionals and public alike to be smitten by the possibilities of the next new pill; an industry unavoidably committed to

5. Angell, *Truth About the Drug Companies*.
6. Doran and Henry, "Disease Mongering," 859.

perpetual innovation as a means for competitive advantage.[7]

Disease mongering can occur in both the physical and mental health industries, but arguably occurs more often in psychiatry. This is because physical illness is more readily detectable through the science of pathology, where clinicians conduct laboratory tests on body fluids, tissue, and cells to detect changes and defects that cause disease. Pathologists use highly advanced and accurate technologies and are able to clearly identify a host of physical problems such as high cholesterol, heart disease, and many forms of cancer.

Many people assume that mental health diagnoses occur in a similar manner, with some form of blood test or similarly biological examination. However that's not the case. The bible for the diagnoses of mental health disorders is called the *Diagnostic and Statistical Manual of Mental Health Disorders* (DSM-5), now in its fifth edition. The title of this book is a bit misleading, as there are no statistics in the manual. Inside is an ever-expanding list of mental health illness classifications, with a series of behavioral symptoms connected with each.

The first DSM was published in 1952 and contained 106 diagnoses and was 130 pages in length. A basic reason for its development was that there was very little unanimity within the profession. Patients might see two different doctors and relay identical symptoms but receive very different treatments. By the time the second edition was published in 1968 the number of disorders had nearly doubled to 182. The DSM-3 arrived in 1980

7. Ibid., 860.

The Manufacturing of Illness

and had reached 265 diagnoses and a length of 494 pages. The more recent edition, DSM-4, came out in 1994 at a length of 886 pages and with just under 300 disorders identified. DSM-5, released in 2013, has grown to over 991 pages and has reclassified numerous disorders, with the total number reaching over 300.

Critics point to the obvious expansion of behaviors that have been classified as "illness" since this highly influential manual was developed. It's not difficult to make the case that virtually every person could qualify as being mentally ill at some point in his or her life using this catalog of disorders. More troubling to the validity of the DSM is the fact that there exist no physical or laboratory tests that can clearly identify a disorder. Instead, members of the DSM committee *vote* on which diagnoses are to be either included or removed. But perhaps the largest criticism of psychiatrists' use of the DSM is the almost exclusive practice of drug therapy to help people who experience problems with living, with almost no consideration for the social, cultural, situational, or spiritual factors that may be influencing mood and behaviors.

The Underlying Causes for Behaviors Overlooked

Before continuing my education so that I might teach at the college level, I worked as a behavioral therapist with children and families, many of whom were prescribed psychotropic medications. Part of the structure of our program was to sit in with our clients when they met with the psychiatrist to assess their progress. I was always taken aback at the very pleasant but surreal nature of these meetings, which occurred every few months during treatment. They were typically quite brief, lasting fifteen minutes or so.

All of them were routine and went very much like this. After pleasantries were exchanged, the psychiatrists would ask how the medications were working. In a few sentences the parents or children would give some generalized feedback, mostly of what occurred during the past few days. They would typically add that the meds either seemed to help or not help. The psychiatrist would then lean back, ask a few more questions, and then collect their thoughts while calmly stroking her or his chin. Then, half talking to themselves and half to their patient, they would review a short list of tweaks in the medication plan, then arrive at a final decision and write the prescription. Lastly there would be a final bit of pleasant chitchat and scheduling for reevaluation in two or three months, and the fifteen minutes were over.

I left these odd meetings with mixed emotions. On one hand there was little doubt that both psychiatrist and patient (or patient's parents or caregiver) were doing their best to be genuine and help or be helped. At the same time to believe that a pill alone can somehow magically fix the intense intergenerational, social, behavioral, relational, and spiritual baggage that tended to haunt these families seemed farcical.

The marketing of drugs has had a profound impact on the way many now view health. Perhaps the most striking example of this for me was a family I worked with who was headed by a just remarried mother of two who struggled with obesity and suffered from depression. There were several clear stressors in her life. In addition

The Manufacturing of Illness

to being a newlywed, both teenage children were getting in trouble at school and home. She had been under the care of a psychiatrist for several years with little if any progress by the time I came to work with her. After some weeks getting to know her and her family, a basic treatment plan was developed, with elemental lifestyle changes. In addition to talk therapy, suggestions included "family night" activities with her children to bring some fun into the home and occasional evening walks for light exercise. While discussing the plan she calmly picked up her prescription of pills and with a wry smile said to me that all she needed was "in this little bottle."

Fortunately the false veneer covering pills is beginning to wear off, as increasing numbers of people are calling out the limits of drug therapy. And the call is coming from many within the profession. Psychiatrist Daniel Carlat's book *Unhinged: The Trouble with Psychiatry— A Doctor's Revelations About a Profession in Crisis* helps us to understand that a pill has a hypnotic effect in part due to the god-like persona attributed to psychiatrists by their patients.

> Patients often view psychiatrists as wizards of neurotransmitters, who can choose just the right medication for whatever chemical imbalance is at play. This exaggerated conception of our capabilities has been encouraged by drug companies, by psychiatrists ourselves, and by our patients' understandable hopes for cures.[8]

In his book, Carlat describes his work. He talks with his patients about their symptoms and then matches

---

8. Carlat, *Unhinged*, 7–8.

those with disorders listed in the DSM. The disorders listed in DSM are broad with a series of checklists for possible symptoms. Patients need to qualify for only a partial listing of symptoms in order to receive a diagnostic label. He argues that strict reliance on the DSM has "drained the color out of the way we understand and treat our patients. It has deemphasized psychological-mindedness, and replaced it with the illusion that we understand our patients when all we are doing is assigning them labels."[9]

These labels help determine which medication to prescribe, to a point. Carlat writes, "To a remarkable degree, our choice of medication is subjective, even random. Perhaps your psychiatrist is in a Lexapro mood this morning, because he was just visited by an attractive Lexapro drug rep."[10] Carlat sums up the problems within the field noting that during the past twenty years:

> Psychiatry has gone astray. We have allowed our treatment decisions to be influenced by the promise of riches from drug companies, rather than by what our patients most need. We have fought pitched turf wars with our colleagues in related disciplines, instead of learning from them . . . Finally, we have unquestioningly sought to become just as "medical" as other doctors, when we should embrace the fact that psychiatry is remarkably different from the rest of medicine.[11]

Carlet is not alone in his experience and thinking. Several authors have written recent and comparable

9. Ibid., 59–60.
10. Ibid., 83.
11. Ibid., 222.

books telling similar stories. These titles include *The Emperor's New Drugs: Exploding the Antidepressant Myth* by Irving Kirsch; *The Loss of Sadness: How Psychiatry Transformed Normal Sorrow into Depressive Disorder* by Allan V. Horwitz and Jerome C. Wakefield; and *Rape of a Soul: How the Chemical Imbalance Model of Modern Psychiatry has Failed its Patients* by Ty Chris Colbert.

Many writers on this subject are sounding the alarm for those in society who are most vulnerable: our children. As drug therapy becomes the treatment of choice for behavioral problems we, as a society, are exposing our youth to a lifetime of medication and self-labeling. And culture is a powerful force. Marilyn Wedge, a family therapist who holds a PhD, points out that here in the United States 9 percent of kids are on drug therapy for ADHD, as compared to a rate of 0.5 percent in France. Why this vast difference? Wedge makes three important distinctions.

First, French child psychiatrists see ADHD as a condition that has not only psychological components, but social and environmental ones as well. So their doctors are much more inclined to consider what social forces are in play that might influence behaviors. Next, Wedge points out that child psychiatrists in France don't follow the DSM, but use an alternative classification that leads doctors to search for underlying causes of behaviors. This enables the professionals to be more holistic in their treatment, looking at factors such as diet, home, school, and community influences that contribute to behaviors.

Lastly, Wedge highlights the cultural differences in parenting. French parents tend to embrace the traditional idea of discipline, motivated by the fact that having healthy expectations for kids doesn't lessen their happiness, but enhances it.

> Consistently enforced limits, in the French view, make children feel safe and secure. Clear limits, they believe, actually make a child feel happier and safer—something that is congruent with my own experience as both a therapist and parent. Finally, French parents believe that hearing the word "no" rescues children from the "tyranny of their own desires" . . . it makes perfect sense to me that French children don't need medications to control their behavior because they learn self-control early in their lives. The children grow up in families in which the rules are well-understood, and a clear family hierarchy is firmly in place.[12]

When sharing this information with my class, the goal is not to try to discern what is and is not a "mental illness," but to expose the powerful and dangerous myth that something outside ourselves alone can "fix us" or make us happy.

---

12. Wedge, "Why French Kids Don't," lines 64–75.

Five

The Futility of Fear

> How strange this fear of death is! We are never frightened at a sunset.
> —George MacDonald (1824–1905)

The rise of medicalization along with an ever-expanding culture of addiction is fueled by a society that is increasingly postmodern and post-natural. The message that permeates from these twin towers in popular culture is fear. Fear of not being cool. Fear of not having enough stuff. Fear of not having enough fun. Fear of aging. Fear of illness and death. This general anxiety is of no value to us, but does effectively convey the misguided idea that just the right combination of products, pills, and pleasures will allow us to leapfrog through life never falling into the icy waters of pain and discomfort.

During the first week of our Sociology of Health and Illness course I introduce students to basic terms. I ask them if they know what morbidity and mortality mean.

Happy Without the Meal

As a group they are typically able to piece together that morbidity refers to illness or injury while mortality refers to death. I then ask:

> Question: What is the mortality rate over the life course for all people who have ever been born? To ask that another way: What percentage of those who have lived on earth experience mortality?
>
> Students often don't quite understand what I'm getting at until I give the answer.
>
> Answer: 100 percent.

The one common experience for everyone who has ever lived is that we are mortal. One day we will die. (Understandably upon beginning such discussions in class I initially receive quite a few blank stares.) Quite naturally college students, like most people, see this as an uncomfortable topic to ponder. What possible purpose could a discussion about death have on health? Actually, a critically important one.

To suppress the realness of perhaps the most profound and certainly inevitable experience we all share by default, leads to the absurd belief that there is no place for suffering in life. Of course no one wants to experience suffering or death, but it is an inevitable and natural part of life. To reflect upon it in a realistic sense cannot but help to put perspective into the purpose and meaning of our existence, both during our earthly lives and, for those who believe in a Supreme Being, our eternal lives. Death can help to "keep it real."

The profoundly challenging reality of death is typically pigeonholed as being relevant only to those who are

The Futility of Fear

"spiritual" or "religious." This social compartmentalization, I would argue, is one of the main reasons our culture has become so dysfunctional. Fortunately there are other voices that value the perspective our mortal nature can offer us.

In *The Heart of Higher Education: A Call to Renewal*, educator Parker Palmer speaks of our mortality as a level that balances everything we do, including of all places, the classroom. He is drawn to the Rule of Benedict, the fourth-century monk and founder of monasteries that conserved much of civilization during intensely harsh periods of history. These monasteries were also forerunners of the modern university emphasis upon books and learning.

> There is much in the Rule of Benedict that I admire, not least Benedict's realism . . . In that same spirit of realism, one of Benedict's rules says, "Daily keep your death before your eyes." When I first read that line at age thirty-five, it struck me as miserably morbid. But as I grew older, I began to realize that it is not morbid at all: rightly understood and practiced, it is a life-giving piece of advice. Cultivating a steady awareness of the fact that we will die can help us savor the gift of life and use it to the fullest.[1]

Being mindful of our mortality can be very positive in a rather practical sense. We know that as far as our bodies are concerned, we live "in time," meaning that even should we live a full life span, we will eventually die. This certainty and perspective can help us to live

---

1. Palmer and Zajonc, *Heart of Higher Education*, 50.

Happy Without the Meal

with simplicity and gratitude, regardless of our chronological age.

> Remember that when you leave this earth you can taken nothing of what you have received, but only what you have a given: a full heart, enriched by honest service, love, sacrifice, and courage.
> —St. Francis of Assisi (1182–1226)

St. Benedict is not at all unusual in the Christian tradition of embracing the truth that we will one day die, and of using this profound reality to bring greater vitality to our lives. In fact this worldview serves as a cornerstone of all the world's great religions that are concerned both with our earthy and eternal lives. Christianity in general and Catholicism in particular have always shed light on the reality of suffering. Like Benedict, virtually all of the saints and Christian apologists sought to find meaning in sorrow and pain.

The Catholic university where I teach is Franciscan, with its heritage and identity inspired by the life of St. Francis of Assisi. St. Francis lived an adventurous and extraordinary life during the twelfth and thirteenth centuries. Many are surprised to learn that this popular saint was first a soldier in his youth. Then as a young man in his early twenties he famously gave up all his possessions, and literally the clothes off his back, to embrace poverty and help the poor in order to serve Christ. St. Francis is well known as a model of peace and for his love of nature.

Francis was a poet-monk and penned his renowned prayer "Canticle of the Sun," which praises God through nature. He saw nature as kin, giving thanks for brother sun, sister moon, brother fire, and mother earth. Francis's life may be most celebrated by scholars for the love he showed to all forms of life. Historian Omer Englebert comments that "biographers of [St. Francis] revert continually to this feeling he had for the beauty of the world and for every living creature."[2]

Francis's reputation for peace and gentleness is often symbolized in statues that grace many landscapes and gardens. A gift from my sister, one stands in my home that depicts Francis gently patting one bird by his chest while another sits on his shoulder. However, like Benedict, this gentle man of peace steadily kept the naked reality of death in his sights. In the same Canticle where he gives thanks to brother sun and mother earth he also adds, "Be praise my Lord for Sister bodily death, from whom no living man can escape." Francis lived his remarkably joyful life not only aware of his mortality, but amidst a life filled with suffering. His disciplines of fasting and self-denial eventually took a toll on his body. He became ill, lost his sight, and received the stigmata, which are painful physical wounds that parallel Jesus' own crucified marks. Yet Francis remained courageous and grateful until the very end of his earthly existence.

Perhaps what makes St. Francis still one of the most beloved saints eight hundred years after his time on earth is his serene acceptance of difficulties. His spirit continues to resonate, especially in today's culture. How can someone be not only happy, but actually joyful without having material things and with experiencing great suf-

---

2. Englebert, *St. Francis of Assisi*, 135.

fering? Another of Francis' biographers shines light on this dichotomy:

> The whole point about St. Francis of Assisi is that he certainly was ascetical and he certainly was not gloomy. As soon as ever he had been unhorsed by the glorious humiliation of his vision of dependence on the divine love, he flung himself into fasting and vigil exactly as he had flung himself furiously into battle. He had wheeled his charger clean round, but there was no halt or check in the thundering impetuosity of his charge. There was nothing negative about it . . . It was not self-denial merely in the sense of self-control. It was as positive as passion; it had all the air of being as positive as pleasure . . . And it is precisely the positive and passionate quality of this part of his personality that is a challenge to the modern mind in the whole problem of the pursuit of pleasure.[3]

Here lays one of the central falsehoods that have seeped into modern culture. The anxious grasping for pleasure and ease at every moment of existence. Denying that pain and suffering is not only a part of our journey but that it can have purpose and meaning. Running away from the inevitable battles in life that challenge us to overcome physical, emotional, social, and spiritual difficulties. Living scared.

The simple realization that life must, by its nature, include suffering has been lost. Like a child going to bed frightened of monsters in the closet, the fear is far worse than the dark room filled with only clothes and toys. This has happened in large part from a false understanding of

---

3. Chesterton, *Saint Thomas Aquinas*, 253–54.

The Futility of Fear

the human psyche. Much of the study of mental health during the past century, while well-intended, has really focused not on mental *health* but mental *illness*. The exclusive attention given to ailments, while noble, has had the unintended consequence that sees suffering in any form as abnormal, if not unnatural.

Victimology Versus Positive Psychology

A primary reason for an almost exclusive focus on mental illness and not mental health was the devastation soldiers experienced during and after World War II. Recognizing the severe impact of those who suffered with combat fatigue, the United States Government established the Veterans Administration in 1946 and pumped into it vast amounts of monies to diagnosis and treat post-traumatic stress disorder, or PTSD. In 1947 the national institute of mental health was founded, offering a great deal of funding for psychological research. The majority of this research focused on illness and not strength. Then in the mid-1950s, pharmaceutical companies began to introduce and promote drugs to be used to treat depression and psychosis, reinforcing a myopic, disease model view of humanity.

However, a major shift in the field occurred in the 1990s, with the emergence of a new branch of mental health called "positive psychology." One of its founders and past president of the American Psychological Association (APA), Martin Seligman recognized how psychology had lost its balance and become "victimology." He writes that psychologists "saw human beings as

Happy Without the Meal

passive foci" where "tissue needs, instincts, and conflicts from childhood pushed each of us around."[4]

Two significant events in Seligman's life are worth noting because they help us understand why psychology has moved in a more engaging and positive direction. The first is academic and sheds light on why many are prone to seeing themselves as victims and therefore seek medicalization. The other is more personal and shows how we can gain wisdom in unexpected ways.

In the 1960s Seligman performed some classic research on animals that gives further insight into this notion of victim stance that can be part of our nature.[5] He conducted a two-part experiment with dogs. In the first part he grouped three dogs in harnesses. Group 1 was bound then simply released. Groups 2 and 3 were yoked together. Group 2 received a mild shock, but could hit a lever and then run free. Group 3 received a similar shock, but the lever did not release the animals. The first two groupings of dogs fully recovered from this experiment, but the third group did not. In fact the dogs showed signs similar to clinical depression, what Seligman would term "learned helplessness."

In part two of his study Seligman placed each of the groupings into a lighted shuttle box, where a low partition divided the container into sections. The light dimmed and ten seconds later a shock was emitted. The dogs merely had to jump to the other side of the box to avoid the mild discomfort. Like part one of the experiment, the first two groups easily moved to the other side and

4. Seligman and Csikszentmihalyi, "Positive Psychology," 6.
5. Seligman and Maier, "Failure to Escape," 1–9.

avoided the shock. However the dogs in Group 3 learned that nothing they did would matter, even though safety was easily within reach. Most of these dogs lay down and whined. Applied to human beings, learned helplessness is a state of mind in which a person is unable or unwilling to avoid negative emotions or consequences, even if they are "escapable."

Out of the Mouth of Babes (Psalm 8:2 NIV)

The second event is an uplifting story involving Seligman and his five-year-old daughter Nikki spending time in their garden. He was working hard weeding while Nikki was having fun, playing and singing as five-year-olds do. He grew agitated, lost his temper and yelled at her. Nikki walked away for a moment then came back to her father and said:

> Daddy, do you remember before my fifth birthday? From the time I was three to the time I was five, I was a whiner. I whined every day. When I turned five, I decided not to whine anymore. That was the hardest thing I've ever done. And if I can stop whining, you can stop being such a grouch.[6]

This past president of the APA describes this moment as an "epiphany, nothing less." In an instant he gained wisdom about himself, his children, and the field of psychology. For himself he learned humility in that yes, he was a grouch, but that he could change. Concerning his daughter, he decided that his focus would be not on

6. Seligman and Csikszentmihalyi, "Positive Psychology," 6.

what's wrong in her actions but on building up what's right. He would focus on her strengths, what he called "seeing into the soul." As to his profession, Seligman realized that one of its key missions—helping to "make the lives of all people more productive and fulfilling"—was almost forgotten.[7]

Seligman, along with a host of other scholars in positive psychology, are now studying qualities such as faith, hope, love, courage, honesty, and perseverance. Until recently these traits were left to the "soft" disciplines of philosophy and theology. Now much of current scientific findings strongly resonate with the wisdom of old and help to see through, and perhaps even be mused at, what passes as freedom and fun in our confused culture.

---

7. Ibid.

Six

Faith, Freedom, and Fun

> I do not find in myself the power to be happy
> merely by doing what I like. On the contrary, if I
> do nothing except what pleases my own fancy
> I will be miserable almost all the time.[1]
>
> —Thomas Merton (1915–1968)

A Fable

There once was a boy who kept sheep not far from the village. He would often become bored and to amuse himself he would call out, "Wolf! Wolf," although there was no wolf about. The villagers would stop what they were doing and run to save the sheep from the wolf's jaw. Once they arrived at the pasture, the boy just laughed. The naughty boy played this joke over and over until the villagers tired of him. One day while the boy was watching the sheep, a wolf did come into the fold. The boy cried and cried, "Wolf!

---

1. Merton, *No Man*, 25.

Wolf!" No one came. The wolf had a feast of sheep that day.[2]

My sense is that we have reached a point in history where we can readily see how false has been the promise of happiness and fulfillment through a life of consumption. *New* discoveries in the social sciences are aligning with *old* teachings from faith traditions and point toward the same true north regarding principles of wellbeing and happiness.

History is marked by people trying to understand how to live "the good life." During this past century marketers have most effectively hijacked the good life, substituting for it "the goods life."[3] Such messaging has been seared into our collective psyche. At the same time the extreme over-promotion of everything, much like the boy who cried wolf, has worn thin.

Early in this book I noted that there is already a great deal of agreement between science and faith on living well. As an example I used the book *Character Strengths and Virtues*, which the authors nickname "a manual of sanities." Here scholars extract six character traits established by research in the social sciences shown to enhance health and happiness. The authors note that these same character strengths align with St. Thomas Aquinas' seven heavenly virtues (wisdom, courage, justice, temperance, faith, hope, and love) from a millennium past. In this chapter I will stick with the lucky number seven, and offer some suggestions for maintaining sanity in the midst of a consumer culture.

2. *Aesop's Fables*, "The Shepherd's Boy."
3. Kasser, "Good Life," 55.

Recognize that Advertisements Are Not Our Reality

> We'll hold the distinction of being the only Nation in the history of the world that ever went to the poor house in an automobile.[4]
>
> —Will Rogers (1879–1935)

Will Rogers, a celebrity entertainer and social commentator was extremely popular during the 1920s and 1930s. Yet even way back then he recognized that our nation had such material abundance that the very nature of being "poor" had changed in our society. Since that time technology, products, and social media have multiplied exponentially. In order to make profits in a saturated market corporations have had to create a phantom of needs.

That's not to say that there is anything inherently unhealthy with buying a hamburger, pair of sneakers, or enjoying some entertainment. Food, clothing, technology, and recreation are certainly good things. However, it's probably also a good idea to be able to see through the oftentimes-silly psychological gimmicks that are attached to these products promising to make us "happy." In reality their goal is to make us emotionally and spiritually devoted to their brand.

One of my son's and my favorite comedians is Jim Gaffigan who has fun with this very idea in one of his routines. He makes light of ways in which our cultural psyche has been branded, in one way or another. Poking at the popularity of McDonald's, he jokes:

---

4. Rogers, "President's Organization on Unemployment."

Happy Without the Meal

> I'm tired of people acting like they're better than McDonald's. You may have never set foot in a McDonald's but you have your own McDonald's. You know instead of maybe buying a Big Mac you read *US Weekly*. Hey that's still McDonald's, it's just served up a little different. Maybe your McDonald's is telling yourself that Starbucks Frappuccino is not a milkshake. Or maybe you watch *Glee*. It's all McDonald's. McDonald's of the soul. Momentary pleasure followed by incredible guilt eventually leading to cancer. "I'm lovin' it."[5]

Like many comedians Gaffigan's humor is funny precisely because it is both mildly humiliating and true for most of us. We do tend to become a bit overly attached to our own brand of stuff. It is rather difficult not to do so living in a consumer culture. But once we become aware of the hooks embedded in the onslaught of advertisements we are again free, no longer being caught up in a confused consumption mentality.

Power Down to Reduce Anxiety

It's very easy to get caught up in the glitter of technology, like the rush of the dopamine-induced loop. Technology and social media are wonderful tools, but they are just tools. They've made life remarkably convenient compared to even the recent past. But it's a dangerous thing to confuse ease with progress. Those who make that mistake risk losing a life of meaning and purpose.

---

5. Gaffigan, "Jim Gaffigan—Mr. Universe."

> It is precisely this illusion, that mechanical progress means human improvement, that alienates us from our own being and our own reality. It is precisely because we are convinced that our life, as such, is better if we have a better car, a better TV set, better toothpaste, etc., that we condemn and destroy our own reality and the reality of our natural resources. Technology was made for man, not man for technology. In losing touch with being and thus with God, we have fallen into a senseless idolatry of production and consumption for their own sakes.[6]

These words from Thomas Merton, written half-century ago and well before the Internet, cell phones, and social media, were prophetic. Social media consumption has arguably surpassed food overconsumption in our country in both quantity and impact. The United States Department of Labor time use survey tells us that Americans watch on average eighty hours of television each month.[7] We're spending increasing amounts of time surfing the Internet on our home computers and smart devices. Young adults are now spending virtually most of the day "online" in some manner.

Numerous articles and books have been written that tease out the negative effects of living a virtual life. The loss of authentic relationships leads to addiction and anxiety. Texts and tweets are great ways to stay in touch, yet when the rush of being connected takes priority over being, we miss out on what we long for.

---

6. Merton, *Conjectures*, 222.
7. Bureau of Labor Statistics, "Leisure Time on an Average Day."

Happy Without the Meal

In 2012 Facebook reported that 83 million users, almost 10 percent of their accounts, were fake.[8] People feel the need to create a persona for a host of reasons, some innocent and some not so innocent. It's important to recognize the simple truth that a virtual life is not a real life. Cyber life doesn't nourish us like real life. It doesn't satisfy. We always want more because there is little and at times no sustenance. We often take for granted those things that are right in front of us, because they're always right in front of us.

If we detach from the need to be constantly keeping up online and relax our grip from the anxiety of the cyber world we will have the time to explore other fun, more natural ways to enjoy spending free time with family and friends. Using technology is good, but we need to savor the real moments and relationships that make for a full and rich life.

Experience the Healing Effects of Nature

> If spring came but once a century instead of once a year, or burst forth with the sound of an earthquake and not in silence, what wonder and expectation there would be in all hearts to behold the miraculous change.
>
> —Henry Wadsworth Longfellow (1807–1882)

A good chunk of my workday is usually taken up responding to emails from students and colleagues, so I limit myself to following one listserv (online discussion

---

8. Thier, "Facebook Profiles are Fake," lines 3–5.

Faith, Freedom, and Fun

group) to keep my screen time manageable. This particular one is for those interested in developments in positive psychology. It's fun to follow the research and work being done in this refreshing new discipline. And there are also exchanges between people in this group that can be very insightful, and in many ways.

A few years ago one member posted a question to the listserv asking if anyone knew of research that supported the notion that it was generally a good thing for kids to grow up near where their grandparents lived. Another member replied that he was a bit jolted that such a question was even asked. He went on to ask in effect, "Do we really need to do a cost/benefit outcome assessment on the role of grandparents?"

The same can be said of nature, being outside. Do we need science to teach us about the benefits of nature? Again, perhaps it's time to see some humor in just how far off course our culture has veered. The cure for so much of what ails us is just out our front doors. And with the rise in social media overconsumption, scholars are increasingly recognizing the fact that, to our peril, we're dismissing the value of nature.

An article titled, "Does Nature 'Minister to the Mind?'" appeared in the journal *BioPsychoSocial Medicine* in 2012. Here the authors review a host of studies that show that nature-related activities are associated with enhanced physical and mental health. They point to the modern trend of kids and adults spending excessive amounts of time online, and too little time outside.

> Excess screen-based media consumption, so-called screen time, may be a driving force in masking awareness of the potential benefits of

Happy Without the Meal

> nature. With global environmental concerns, rapid urban expansion, and mental health disorders at crisis level, diminished nature contact may not be without consequences to the health of the individual and the planet itself.[9]

This disconnect with nature leading to its many troubling consequences has been summed up by the phrase, "nature deficit disorder." This is not a literal mental health condition, but a saying coined by Richard Louv as an explanation for the increasing distance between people and nature. This loss of connection with sun and air, fun and play has had very harmful effects on our health in virtually every dimension. Louv points out that several converging social factors have emerged, separating folks from the great outdoors and its many health benefits.

> In the 1970s, the physical and academic designs of too many school districts turned inward, resulting in the building of windowless schools, the banishment of animals from classrooms, and even the elimination of recess and field trips. Several forces have been at work. Within schools, these forces include the wave of well-intentioned and underfunded education reforms. Beyond the schools, they include poor urban design, disappearing open space, parental fear of "stranger danger," amplified news cycles and sensationalized entertainment media, competition from computers and video games, the overstructuring of childhood, and the devaluing of natural play.[10]

---

9. Logan and Selhub, "Does Nature?," 1.
10. Louv, "Do Our Kids?," 26–27.

Faith, Freedom, and Fun

Of these seven suggestions, this is the most challenging to write about because it is so self-evident. Like most families, mine has filled albums, cell phones, and hard drives with seemingly endless photos. As I look at the ones tacked to our walls and covering our fridge, at least half are of people spending time together outside. My family is drawn to a variety of sports. My daughters' favorites are basketball and gymnastics, my son's is football, and my wife and I love to run and play golf. The competition adds some spice, but the point is to get outside and let the sun and air heal and refresh.

Some years ago my sister gave me a book of brief daily reflections called *God Calling*. The one for August 17 is titled "Nature Laughs," and in part reads:

> Live much out here. My sunshine, my glorious air, my presence, my teaching. Would they not make holiday anywhere for you. Sunshine helps to make glad the heart of man. It is the laughter of nature. Live much outside. My medicines are sun and air, trust and faith. . . . Nature is often my nurse for tired souls and weary bodies. Let her have her way with you.[11]

If you are already into the outdoors I bet these words resonate with you. If you're not familiar with spending time outside, give it a try. Even a little walk in the neighborhood, in a park, or the woods is a great start. You may be surprised how something so simple can make us feel so good.

---

11. Russell, *God Calling*, 161.

Happy Without the Meal

Practice Faith for a Happier Life

> There are only two ways to live your life. One is as though nothing is a miracle. The other is as though everything is a miracle.
>
> —Albert Einstein (1879–1955)

We live in an increasingly irreligious society in spite of the fact that even secular, academic research consistently finds that people who practice faith are happier than those who do not.[12] A Gallup poll published in 2012 found that Americans who are religious enjoy higher levels of wellbeing than their less religious neighbors.

> An analysis of more than 676,000 Gallup-Healthways Well-Being Index interviews conducted in 2011 and 2010 finds that Americans who are the most religious have the highest levels of wellbeing. The statistically significant relationship between religiousness and wellbeing holds up after controlling for numerous demographic variables.[13]

Most research in this area rightly notes the difference between "religion" and "spirituality." Religion refers to the structure and organized manner in which faith is practiced. Spirituality denotes more of the experience or sense of being connected to something beyond the self. These are important scholarly distinctions, but have had the unintended consequences of promoting the popular adage, "I'm spiritual but not religious."

---

12. Holder et al., "Spirituality, Religiousness, and Happiness," 131; Koenig, *Faith and Mental Health*.

13. Newport et al., "Religious Americans," lines 1–4.

Faith, Freedom, and Fun

It is certainly the case that, as shown in the life of St. Francis, God can be found everywhere and in all of creation. At the same time denying the role of any structure to the practice of faith makes it not so much spirituality as it does fleeting, emotionalized experiences. In class I use the analogy that spirituality without any structure is like playing a sport without any rules. The game can quickly become chaotic and meaningless as players each make up their own rulebook.

We talk a good deal about these differences in our Social Psychology of Addictions class, where the field of addictions is oftentimes connected with spirituality and the recovery program Alcoholics Anonymous (AA). The famous psychiatrist Carl Jung was influential in the founding of AA, and coined the adage *Spiritus contra Spiritum*. This Latin phrase means "alcoholism countered," or "defeated by spirituality." Alcoholics Anonymous is a spiritual program not affiliated with any religion, but it certainly has a great deal of structure, not least of which are the twelve steps and twelve traditions. When discussing spirituality and religion in class we come full circle, noting that ultimately these two concepts, while technically distinct, naturally overlap. Religion is a structured way to seek the spiritual. Spirituality is the pursuit of the sacred in life, but if only sought for personal experience or pleasure will likely lead to selfishness and egotism.

Harold Koenig MD, professor of psychiatry and behavioral sciences at Duke University Medical Center, has conducted extensive research and written at length on the intersection of religion and wellbeing. In his book *Faith and Mental Health: Resources for Healing*, Koenig reviews the academic research on the intersection of faith and wellbeing, and offers a simple conclusion: the vast majority of studies support the traditional notion that faith enhances wellbeing and happiness.

> Religious beliefs and practices are inversely associated with anxiety and depression in the majority of cross-sectional studies, usually predict less depression and faster recovery from depression in prospective studies, and, when examined in randomized clinical trials, religious interventions cause a faster reduction in clinical symptoms than secular therapies alone or no treatment. This is also true, in general, for negative character personality traits, antisocial activities that involve crime or delinquency, and use of drugs or alcohol. Thus, while not all studies report mental health benefits from religion, the vast majority of both qualitative and quantitative studies do.[14]

I would bet most of us don't have to look far to find people who exemplify what Koenig's research confirms. For me that person is my mom. Though just a gentle, uncomplicated woman, she navigated her way through life guided by faith and reason. Mom is one of the most real persons I've ever known. As far as religion goes she never preached to us about faith, but just taught us and then lived it. Those who know her would agree that her presence was like the famous saying attributed to St. Francis, "Preach the gospel at all times. If necessary, use words."

A few years ago, before dementia took much of her memory, we were sitting at her kitchen table having a lighthearted conversation. Then eighty-four years old, she still had a remarkable tranquility and joy about her.

14. Koenig, *Faith and Mental Health*, 112.

Faith, Freedom, and Fun

During our chat she became a bit reflective and said, "Life goes so fast." To that I replied, "Coming up on your eighty-fifth birthday, what would you share with others about life?" She got out half a sentence, "Oh, I don't know, . . ." but then in a flash declared, "Just appreciate what you have in life. Be grateful."

It's funny how an old, simple little Irish woman could distill principles of wellbeing *newly* discovered by social scientists. On page 553 of the 800-page text *Character Strengths and Virtues*, scholars present research findings that establish gratitude as a character trait scientifically shown to enhance happiness and wellbeing. Here they cite the work of G. K. Chesterton from his book *Orthodoxy*, which was published twenty-five years before my mom was born.

> The test of all happiness is gratitude. Children are grateful when Santa Claus puts in their stockings gifts of toys or sweets. Could I not be grateful to Santa Claus when he puts in my stockings the gift of two miraculous legs? We thank people for birthday presents . . . Can I thank no one for the birthday present of birth?[15]

Theses scholars go on to explain that while new research is confirming the positive effects of having a grateful outlook, not many studies have been done on this virtue.

> Over the years, mainstream social science has been somewhat neglectful of the concept of gratitude. Negative psychological states such as anger, depression and anxiety have generated literally thousands of scientific research proj-

---

15. Peterson and Seligman, *Character Strengths*, 553.

> ects. Research that has specifically focused on gratitude of thankfulness, on the other hand, is limited.... Much of what we have learned about gratitude reflects research conducted within the very recent past. Therefore, much is not known.[16]

Fortunately research into how faith has conventionally been taught by faith traditions continues to confirm what has been handed down from generation to generation. The emerging field of positive psychology is among the leading areas in science that conducts research on living a rich, joy-filled life. In 2007 the groundbreaking work *The How of Happiness* was published and claimed to be the first book to scientifically show how people can live happier. Author Sonya Lyubomirsky offers twelve activities, based on research, which have been shown to make folks happier. Among these include expressing gratitude, having good relationships with friends and family, learning to forgive, living in the moment, and savoring life's simply joys. Clearly many of these activities align with traditional faith practices.

Though a scientific work on good mental health, Lyubomirsky dedicates one of the activities to practicing religion and spirituality, and highlights research findings that indicate religious people are happier than those who are nonreligious. When explaining why this is the case she rejects the notion that religion makes people happier just because they hang out with likeminded people. She offers some insightful reasoning that helps to explain this relationship.

16. Ibid., 567.

Faith, Freedom, and Fun

First, a person's actual relationship with God is the real experience of a bond. Not unlike that between a father and son, mother and daughter, or best friends. There is a belief and reality that we are in communion with a Supreme Being who has created us for happiness here on earth and for eternity after we die. Lyubomirsky writes, "Those of you who feel this way have a sense of security that others only wish for."[17]

Second, the reason religion leads to happiness is that people of faith recognize that life will not be like a Coke commercial. We all experience ordinary, and at times difficult, periods in life. Having faith gives perspective that while we may not understand why something bad happens, we can trust that God will use those times somehow for good. Lyubomirsky goes so far as to state, "This is critical. Regardless of whether you are involved with a formal religious organization, your health and happiness may benefit simply (or perhaps not so simply) from your having religious faith. This becomes particularly important during challenging times."[18]

Lastly, Lyubomirsky points out that the practice of faith is quite simply related to a wide range of positive emotions that are associated with happiness. She writes that "private prayer, spiritual pursuit, and collective worship—can engender hope, gratitude, love, awe, compassion, joy, and even ecstasy, all being happiness-increasing feelings."[19]

---

17. Lyubomirsky, *How of Happiness*, 230.
18. Ibid.
19. Ibid., 232.

Happy Without the Meal

Lymbrosky does a very nice job of summing up the wide range of emotions related to religions, such as Christianity. However if there is one that I would add to her list it would be laughter and just having fun. Perhaps the greatest misconception about Christianity in general, and Catholicism in particular, is that it promotes a gloomy, suppressed way of living. I've found just the opposite is true.

Enjoy More with Less

> In Catholicism, the pint, the pipe
> and the Cross can all fit together.
> —G. K. Chesterton (1874–1936)

Writing this book has been fun in part because of the challenging topic. The title *Happy Without the Meal* conveys the message that we can find happiness in ways other than consumption. Added to that is the notion that overconsumption actually lessens our wellbeing instead of increasing happiness. At the same time there is the risk of implying that the things we consume or do are of themselves unhealthy for us. That's certainly not the case.

This misconception occurred a few years ago with one of my students in our addictions class. We had finished with the first part of the course covering alcohol and other drugs and were just getting into behavioral addictions and speaking about the dangers of things like compulsive shopping, emotional eating, and spending too much time on social media sites. A very bright young woman spoke up in class and said, "You just don't want our generation to have any fun." What a fantastic

Faith, Freedom, and Fun

statement! And one that led to some really honest and interesting discussions over the next few weeks. This wonderful feedback helped me rethink and rework how to begin this section of the course, as that was precisely the *opposite* of the message I am trying to convey.

One of the lessons I've learned from my family, faith, and profession is the especially important role that fun play has in living a good and happy life. The sad irony is that continually chasing fun and amusement for its own sake (the core message in popular culture) soon destroys the very thing pursued. Going back to the young lady in class, I remember sharing with her and the class that not only do I want them to have fun, but that as it relates to health, we know quite well that fun (entertainment, pleasure, joy) is most definitely a good thing as it nourishes body, mind, and soul.

As a Catholic college professor it is very refreshing to see psychologists begin to examine the role of faith in people's lives. Historically psychology has been antagonistic and, at times openly hostile, toward religion and spirituality.[20] Add this to the media's portrayal of religious folks as being unsophisticated, and this has created a difficult culture for people to be strong in their faith and wellbeing.

> Wherever the Catholic sun doth shine,
> There's always laughter and good red wine.
> At least I've always found it so. Benedicamus Domino!
>
> —Hilaire Belloc (1870–1953)

---

20. Elenchin, *Hidden Courage*, 11–39.

Happy Without the Meal

I will double-down on my wager from a few pages ago and again bet that most of us can recall religious folks who had childlike spirits, and were anything but dull and uninteresting. Those who had lightness about them and a hair trigger for fun and laughter. I've had the good fortune to know probably more than my fair share, but the person who stands out would be my dad.

He loved to be around people, to do things, and have fun. In high school he excelled in sports and, after serving in World War II, played several more years of minor league baseball with the Chicago White Sox and Boston Red Sox farm clubs. In addition to raising his kids he also spent seemingly endless years coaching little league baseball. At age forty-five he helped start a hunting club with most of the other members being half his age. He took up the game of golf at age sixty-five and would still run (literally run) with his grandkids into his late seventies.

Dad loved to have fun. One of his favorite traditions happened during Christmas and Easter holidays after my siblings and I were pretty much grown. By late morning about a dozen of his friends would drop by and enjoy a few beers and a whole lot of laughter down in his cellar before the main meal of the day. And by laughter I don't mean the kind you hear piped into the background of sitcoms on TV. This was that full-bodied, eyes-tearing, belly laughter that overflows into delight. Being stationed with the Army in Germany for several years I missed some of those gatherings, but still have great memories of the times I was able to make it home. Fun was as much a part of my dad's faith as was any other part.

Jesuit priest and author James Martin wrote a wonderful book amusingly titled, *Between Heaven and Mirth:*

Faith, Freedom, and Fun

Why Joy, Humor, and Laughter Are at the Heart of the Spiritual Life, which speaks precisely to how my dad lived. Father James points to the misconception regarding the importance of fun and laughter among people of faith, who oftentimes see religion in an exclusively serious manner. He does a great job of showing how the Scriptures as well as the saints (typically portrayed as somber half-human statues) radiate not only joy, but those normal ways humans experience joy, such as making jokes, having fun, teasing friends, and enjoying company, humor, and laughter. Most of the saints did all of these things and had a genuine but happy outlook on life.

St. Thomas Aquinas said, "Joy is the noblest human act," St. Francis De Sales noted that "A sad saint is a sad sort of saint," while Proverb 17:22 counsels, "A cheerful heart is a good medicine, but a downcast spirit dries up the bones." Some saints were even able to express humor in what could be called a heroic manner. Chancellor of England during the rule of Henry VIII, St. Thomas More was sentenced to death by the guillotine for not condoning Henry's divorce. Climbing the step to reach the platform where he would lose his head, More said to the executioner, "See me safe up: for in my coming down I can shift for myself."[21]

The funny Father traces this important and enjoyable virtue all the way back to the founder of Christianity.

> Joy brackets Jesus's life on earth. At the beginning of his life, after the annunciation, Mary goes to Elizabeth. What happens? John the Baptist leaps for joy in Elizabeth's womb. And what does Mary do? She sings a song of praise.

21. As cited in Martin, *Between Heaven and Mirth*, 96.

Happy Without the Meal

> "My soul magnifies the Lord, and my spirit rejoices in god my Savior." At the end of Jesus's earthly life, after the Resurrection, the Risen Christ is grilling some fish on the shore. Peter sees him from a boat and leaps into the water for joy. Joy also kicks off Jesus's public ministry. What is traditionally called the first miracle happens in Cana, where Jesus miraculously turns water into wine, thus making sure that the party will continue. Joy is an essential element of the life and ministry of Jesus. So should it be for any of his followers.[22]

What great advice! Fun and laughter should bracket our lives as well, companying us from cradle to grave. As children most of us never needed to read a book or hear a lecture on how to have fun. Play and laughter came as naturally as the hunger and thirst that followed energetic play. But also for many of us as we've aged we may have begun to take ourselves a bit too seriously and have lost the idea of being joyful and having a happy disposition. If so, maybe it's time to recapture the lessons of youth and enjoy our journey through this life.

"A DISCIPLINED MIND LEADS TO HAPPINESS"
—DALAI LAMA

> Seek freedom and become captive of your desires.
> Seek discipline and find your liberty.
> —FRANK HERBERT (1920–1986)

---

22. Ibid., 207.

Faith, Freedom, and Fun

If there's one word that embodies the polar opposite of the messaging emitted from a consumer culture it may be "discipline." In a materialist society the term has an almost vulgar ring to it. After all, we have all these products to choose from that have been specifically designed to take care of our health and happiness. We would have to be dim-witted to think there's any relevance in such a dated concept. This is one of the reasons why discipline conjures up the notion of pain, self-denial, or even punishment. Decades ago Fulton Sheen picked up on this and said, "Why are those who are notoriously undisciplined and unmoral also most contemptuous of religion and morality? They are trying to solace their own unhappy lives by pulling the happy down to their own abysmal depths."[23]

In a few of the courses I teach related to wellness we talk about the difference between discipline and punishment. When we begin I break up the class into groups and ask the students to see if they can come up with a definition and a few key distinctions between these two terms. Initially the students struggle a bit to find much difference. To help make the distinction we look at the origin of the words.

The word "punish" can be traced to the Latin *punier*, which refers to pain or penalty, and *punire*, meaning to "inflict a penalty on, cause pain for some offense." So punishment is a negative term and refers to inflicting hurt or extracting revenge from a person or thing.

The word "discipline" is quite different. Traced to the Latin *diciplina*, it means "instruction given, teaching,

---

23. Sheen, *Seven Words of Jesus*, 83.

Happy Without the Meal

learning, knowledge." The related term *discipulus* means "pupil." Discipline is positive and brings to mind school, education, and training of self or others.[24] In Christianity the word "disciple" is also from this same root word, meaning "student" or "follower."

Going back to the origin and literal meaning of words can be eye opening. In this same class we make a further connection by looking at the word "school." School is traced to the Greek *skhole*, meaning "leisure" and "spare time." The earliest scholars, who date back as early as sixth-century BC, were those lucky few who were not preoccupied with the daylong grind of hunting and gathering.

In today's society we have largely lost the idea that school is a time of leisure. Sadly it is often a stress-filled experience for not only students, but teachers as well. From a cultural viewpoint the same negative connotation applies to discipline as well. And the two are related. School, although for most a "spare time" of rest away from employment to learn still requires work and effort. Inherently school not only requires discipline but is itself a discipline.

We've likely heard the common and, I believe true, sayings "we never stop learning," and "school of life," or "university of hard knocks." These sayings hit home to me when I was about to complete and then defend my PhD dissertation. I began these studies in my late thirties while working and raising a family. Three grueling years

24. *Online Etymology Dictionary*, "punish," http://www.etymonline.com/index.php?allowed_in_frame=0&search=punish&searchmode=none, and "discipline," http://www.etymonline.com/index.php?allowed_in_frame=0&search=discipline&searchmode=none.

Faith, Freedom, and Fun

later and with graduation in sight, my mentor said to me, "Earning your PhD isn't the end, it's the beginning." At first that stung a bit because I was so ready (I mean *really* ready) to be done. But soon the message hit home. Of course, it wasn't the end at all. Sure, one leg of the journey was over, but now it was time to start anew.

Discipline, in its truest sense, is a critically important trait to develop, especially in a culture that mocks this quality. However, discipline does not mean perfection. We're all human. No one is disciplined in every area of their lives. I've come to increasingly appreciate this quality and encourage my children to develop this trait as well. Discipline is one of the common themes that underlie virtually all pursuits in life. From business, to education, to family life, to health, or sports, this trait is foundational. The practice of any faith system requires this as well. In his book *The Art of Happiness*, Dalai Lama XIV writes:

> Whether our action is wholesome or unwholesome depends on whether that action or deed arises from a disciplined or undisciplined state of mind. It is felt that a disciplined mind leads to happiness and an undisciplined mind leads to suffering, and in fact it is said that bringing about discipline within one's mind is the essence of the Buddha's teaching.[25]

It's not very difficult to see why discipline leads to happiness or why a lack of discipline leads to suffering. If there are little or no structures or formative habits in our lives we are at the mercy of what an ever-changing culture

25. Dalai Lama and Cutler, *Art of Happiness*, 46.

tells us is true. Like the dated but spot-on saying goes, "if you don't stand for something you'll fall for anything."

A few years ago I taught an Introduction to Sociology course. As part of the course I introduced students to the difference between scholarly, peer reviewed journal articles and nonacademic writings. Academic articles are original works by scholars who support their ideas or research findings by citing what's been established in the literature (previous academic work done on the subject). These articles are commonly peer reviewed where a panel of experts provides feedback prior to that article being accepted for publication. Scholarly journals are easy to recognize by their studious titles such as *Journal of the American Medical Association* and *Journal for the Scientific Study of Religion*.

Popular magazine articles are those written by journalists who work as reporters covering news and current events. These pieces are typically reviewed by magazine editors and then published. Popular magazines are those such as *Newsweek*, *Sports Illustrated*, and *National Geographic*. Neither scholarly nor popular articles are "better" than the other, as they serve different purposes.

In the introductory course the students were to complete a simple project. Select any topic they were interested in related to sociology and locate three scholarly articles on the subject area. They were to write a brief paper and give a presentation to class based on the information they learned from reading the articles.

A very personable young man in his junior year had selected the topic of sex and college-aged students. Shortly into his presentation he said, "As we all know everyone has had sex by the time they reach college," and then continued speaking. I was stunned! I interrupted his presentation and asked if this "fact" was based on research or his own opinion. He said research. He was wrong. (A 2011 Centers for Disease Control and Prevention study found that roughly half of all high school students had not engaged in sexual activity.[26])

After class we spoke and I asked him to bring me the articles. He did have articles related to his topic area but of course none of them hinted at the notion that by the time students reach college they've all had intimate physical relationships. He told me that he just assumed that was the case because of his own experiences. I'm convinced the young man had no intention of being dishonest in his presentation, but he was certainly undisciplined in his effort.

> Some people regard discipline as a chore.
> For me, it is a kind of order that sets me free to fly.
> —JULIE ANDREWS (1935–)

When you come right down to it, we really can't accomplish anything worthwhile without some type of practice, training, or learning. Playing sports, training for a marathon, studying for a career all take effort but are at the same time fun—if we're willing to see them that way. They can be fun precisely because discipline leads to freedom. Laurence Boldt brings home this point:

> Discipline is simply a matter of doing what we must, without wasting time or energy worrying about whether or not we like it. When we de-

---

26. Centers for Disease Control, "Adolescent and School Health," line 4.

> velop the habit of plunging in without whining, complaining, or procrastinating, we are on our way to genuine freedom.[27]

Modern research in the social sciences has discovered and is championing a similar trait now termed "resilience." Resilience refers to the ability be able to "bounce back" when things don't go our way. To not let adversity keep us down, but to overcome the challenges and setbacks that at times happen in life. This concept has become quite popular during the past few years with programs being developed for children, college students, and even military personnel.

The American Psychological Association has a website offering ten tips for building resilience in children and teenagers.[28] These disciplines include having good relationships at home and school, developing a daily routine, eating well and getting exercise, developing goals, and accepting the notion that change is part of life.

The University of Pennsylvania Positive Psychology Center has developed a resilience training program for the United States Army called the Comprehensive Soldier Fitness. This program teaches service members how to be strong by highlighting five dimensions of strength—physical, emotional, social, family, and spiritual—and teaches soldiers ways to fortify these areas.[29] The renowned Mayo Clinic offers resilience training aimed to help people find meaning in life, develop gratitude, and address spirituality needs.[30] The growing popularity of

27. Boldt, *Zen Soup*, 110.
28. American Psychological Association, "Resilience Guide," 2.
29. United States Army, "Building Resilience."
30. Mayo Clinic, "Resilience," lines 1–8.

Faith, Freedom, and Fun

these kinds of programs is a hopeful sign that our society is regaining perspective and practical antidotes to the materialist mindset.

Listen to Youth and Learn

> Do not become upset when difficulty comes your way. Laugh in its face and know that you are in the arms of God.[31]
> —St. Francis de Sales (1567–1622)

Abraham Lincoln is reported to have mused that "people are about as happy as they make up their minds to be," and to a large degree I think that's true. However it's not hard to argue that it's becoming harder for folks to make up their minds to be happy. Our culture has continually devolved into a technical and materialistic wasteland marked by fear. Pope John Paul II famously coined the phrase "culture of death," capturing what so many now feel and experience. In his encyclical *Evangelium Vitae* (Gospel of Life) he writes:

> This reality is characterized by the emergence of a culture which denies solidarity and in many cases takes the form of a veritable "culture of death." This culture is actively fostered by powerful cultural, economic and political currents which encourage an idea of society excessively concerned with efficiency. Looking at the situation from this point of view, it is possible to speak in a certain sense of *a war of the powerful against the weak* . . . A person who, because of

---

31. As cited in Martin, *Between Heaven and Mirth*, 174.

> illness, handicap or, more simply, just by existing, compromises the well-being or life-style of those who are more favoured tends to be looked upon as an enemy to be resisted or eliminated. In this way a kind of "*conspiracy against life*" is unleashed.[32]

While writing this book, in fact this very chapter, my thirteen-year-old took her first trip to New York City with two parish priests and a small group of girls from other parishes. The purpose of the August trip was to see the perpetual vows of nuns from the Sisters of Life. The trip lasted three days, giving the girls time to have fun shopping in the city and to take in a Broadway show. When my daughter came home she excitedly told us all about her trip. Other than the summer heat she had nothing but good things to say about her time in the city. But the following day she had an interesting reflection. "Dad," she said, "I really had a great time. I love New York! But it was really sort of weird how so many people seemed so sad. And angry."

Those words struck me. Why is it that so many of us are sad though we live amidst material abundance? In part it is because of such abundance. Stephen Rossetti, in his book *When the Lion Roars*, reflects on Jesus' teaching, "Whoever seeks to preserve his life will lose it, but whoever loses it will save it" (Luke 17:33 NAB). Rossetti tells us that fear of not having enough (even though we live with excess) makes us cling even tighter to the desire for more. Instead of leading to satisfaction it leads to greater anxiety.

---

32. Pope John Paul II, *Gospel of Life*, 22.

Faith, Freedom, and Fun

He then relays his own experience, which mirrors my daughter's. Rossetti spent time away from society on retreat with Carthusian monks. On his return to the "world" he made this observation:

> Riding on a public bus, I was immediately struck with the pervasive sadness that surrounded and permeated the people on the bus. They were heavily weighed down by their joyless world. The saddest thing is that they did not recognize what they had lost; they apparently believed that their life was "normal." I had only come to recognize this horrible sadness after having experienced the joy exuded by the monks. Their eleventh-century founder, Bruno, described their life as "a peace unknown to the world, and joy in the Holy Spirit."[33]

The point of Rossetti's experience is not to suggest that we need to join a religious order to find happiness. But it does serve to highlight the notion that we have reached a point where the social sciences empirically confirm what Christianity has long proclaimed. Both are in agreement that genuine, lasting happiness can't be bought, eaten, or somehow consumed.

> To have courage for whatever comes in life—
> everything lies in that.
> —St. Teresa of Avila (1515–1582)

Although we live in a culture that often promotes anxiety as a ploy to generate business, we do have the ability to see through the ruse. It takes courage to be hon-

---

33. Rossetti, *When the Lion Roars*, 131.

est with ourselves, and to see if we're using things or if we're the ones being used. We all have that ability, but it may take some practice; that combined with being aware of the times and culture we live in. We can enjoy what the world has to offer without losing our real freedom. Yes we can be happy, even without the meal.

Bibliography

The American Chesterton Society. "Quotations of G. K. Chesterton." No pages. Online http://www.chesterton.org/discover-chesterton/quotations-of-g-k-chesterton/.

The American Psychological Association. "Resilience Guide for Parents and Teachers." No pages. Online: http://www.apa.org/helpcenter/resilience.aspx

Angell, Marcia. *The Truth About the Drug Companies: How They Deceive Us and What to Do About It*. New York: Random House, 2004.

Barr, Stephen. *Modern Physics and Ancient Faith*. Notre Dame, IN: University of Notre Dame Press, 2003.

Bloch, Michael. "Fast Facts—Consumption Statistics." Green Living Tips, May 4, 2012. No pages. Online: http://www.greenlivingtips.com/articles/185/1/Consumption-statistics.html.

Boldt, Laurence G. *Zen Soup: Tasty Morsels of Wisdom from Great Minds East and West*. New York: Penguin, 1997.

Bunker, John P., et al. "Improving Health: Measuring Effects of Medical Care." *Milbank Quarterly* 72, no. 2 (1994) 225–58.

Bureau of Labor Statistics. "American Time Use Survey Summary." American Time Use Survey, United States Department of Labor, 2011. No pages. Online: http://www.bls.gov/tus/charts/.

Bureau of Labor Statistics. "Leisure Time on an Average Day." American Time Use Survey, United States Department of Labor, 2011. No pages. Online: http://www.bls.gov/tus/charts/chart9.pdf.

Campbell, James C. "Parable of a Goose." Sunday sermon, St. Eulalia Parish, Coudersport, PA, January 2011.

Campaign for a Commercial-Free Childhood. "Marketing to Children Overview." No pages. Online: http://www.commercialfreechildhood.org/resource/marketing-children-overview.

Bibliography

Carlat, Daniel. *Unhinged: The Trouble with Psychiatry—A Doctor's Revelations About a Profession in Crisis*. New York: Free Press, 2010.

Carroll, Andrew, ed. "The Indians of the Six Nations to William & Mary College on Why They Will Not Be Sending Their Boys to the College." In *Letters of a Nation*, 240. New York: Kodansha America, 1990.

Catechism of the Catholic Church. Liguori, MO: Liguori, 1994.

Centers for Disease Control and Prevention. "Adolescent and School Health." No Pages. Online: http://www.cdc.gov/healthyyouth/sexualbehaviors/index.htm.

Chesterton, G. K. *Saint Thomas Aquinas/Saint Francis of Assisi*. San Francisco: Ignatius, 2002.

———. "The Suicide of Thought." In *Orthodoxy*, chap. 3. No pages. Online: http://www.leaderu.com/cyber/books/orthodoxy/ch3.html.

Conrad, Peter. *The Medicalization of Society*. Baltimore, MD: Johns Hopkins, 2007.

Dalai Lama, and Howard C. Cutler. *The Art of Happiness: A Handbook For Living*. New York: Riverhead, 1998.

Davis, Sue. "Marketing of Foods to Children: A New Language." *Education Review* 19, no. 2 (2006) 40–48.

Demille, Cecil B. Commencement Address, Brigham Young University, May 31, 1957. *Conference Reports* (October 1959) 127.

Dokoupil, Tony. "Is the Onslaught Making Us Crazy?" *Newsweek* (July 16, 2012) 24–30.

Doran, E., and D. Henry. "Disease Mongering: Expanding the Boundaries of Treatable Disease." *Internal Medicine Journal* 32 (2008) 858–61.

Elenchin, William J. *Hidden Courage: Reconnecting Faith and Character with Mental Wellness*. Eugene, OR: Wipf and Stock, 2009.

Englebert, Omer. *St. Francis of Assisi: A Biography*. Ann Arbor, MI: Servant, 1965.

Franklin, Benjamin. "Proposals Relating to the Education of Youth in Pensilvania." Penn University Archives and Records Center. No pages. Online: http://www.archives.upenn.edu/primdocs/1749proposals.html.

Freedhoff, Yoni, and Arya M. Sharma. "'Lose 40 Pounds in 4 Weeks': Regulating Commercial Weight-Loss Programs." *Canadian Medical Association Journal* 180, no. 4 (February 17, 2009) 367.

Bibliography

Fryar, Cheryl D., Margaret D. Carroll, and Cynthia L. Ogden. "Prevalence of Overweight, Obesity, and Extreme Obesity Among Adults: United States, Trends 1960–1962 Through 2009–2010." Centers for Disease Control and Prevention, Division of Health and Nutrition Examination Surveys. No pages. Online: http://www.cdc.gov/nchs/data/hestat/obesity_adult_09_10/obesity_adult_09_10.htm.

Gaffigan, Jim. "Jim Gaffigan—Mr. Universe—'McDonald's.'" YouTube. Video file 9:02, May 11, 2012. Online: http://www.youtube.com/watch?v=6YDTfEhChgw.

Grassie, William. "Postmodernism: What One Needs to Know." *Zygon* 32, no. 1 (March 1997) 83–94.

Hamilton, Clive, and Richard Denniss. *Affluenza: When Too Much is Never Enough*. Crows Nest NSW, Australia: Allen & Unwin, 2005.

High-Tech Productions. "The History of Film, Television and Video." No pages. Online: http://www.high-techproductions.com/historyoftelevision.htm

Holder, Mark D., et al. "Spirituality, Religiousness, and Happiness in Children Aged 8–12." *Journal of Happiness Studies* 11 (2010) 131–50.

Jenaro, Christina, et al. "Problematic Internet and Cell-Phone Use: Psychological, Behavioral, and Health Correlates." *Addiction Research and Theory* 15, no. 3 (January 18, 2007) 309–20.

Kang, Cecilia. "Number of Cellphones Exceeds U.S. Population: CTIA Trade Group." *Washington Post*, October 11, 2011, Business, http://www.washingtonpost.com/blogs/post-tech/post/number-of-cell-phones-exceeds-us-population-ctia-trade-group/2011/10/11/gIQARNcEcL_blog.html.

Kasser, Tim. "The Good Life or the Goods Life? Positive Psychology and Personal Well-Being in the Culture of Consumption." In *Positive Psychology in Practice*, edited by P. Alex Linley and Stephen Joseph, 55–67. Hoboken, NJ: John Wiley, 2004.

King, Martin Luther, Jr. "Letter from Birmingham Jail." The Martin Luther King, Jr. Research and Education Institute, Stanford University. No pages. Online: http://mlk-kpp01.stanford.edu/index.php/resources/article/annotated_letter_from_birmingham/.

Koenig, Harold. *Faith and Mental Health: Religious Resources for Healing*. West Conshohocken, PA: Templeton, 2005.

Lewis, C. S. *Mere Christianity*. New York: HarperCollins, 1952.

———. *Weight of Glory*. New York: Macmillan, 1949.

Bibliography

Lewis, Harry R. *Excellence Without a Soul: Does Liberal Education Have a Future?* New York: Public Affairs, 2006.

Logan, Alan C., and Eva M. Selhub. "Vis Medicatrix Natureae: Does Nature 'Minister to the Mind?'" *BioPsychoSocial Medicine* 6, no. 11 (2012) 1–10.

Lone Star College–Kingwood. "American Cultural History 1940–1949." No pages. Online: http://kclibrary.lonestar.edu/decade40.html.

Louv, Richard. "Do Our Kids Have Nature-Deficit Disorder?" *Health and Learning* 67, no. 4 (2009) 24–30.

Lucas, Christopher J. *American Higher Education: A History.* 2nd ed. New York: Palgrave Macmillan, 2006.

Lyubomirsky, Sonya. *The How of Happiness: A Scientific Approach to Getting the Life You Want.* New York: Penguin, 2007.

Martin, James. *Between Heaven and Mirth: Why Joy, Humor, and Laughter Are at the Heart of the Spiritual Life.* New York: HarperCollins, 2011.

Mayo Clinic. "Resilience: Build Skills to Endure Hardship." Adult Health. No Pages. Online: http://www.mayoclinic.com/health/resilience/MH00078/NSECTIONGROUP=2.

McKeown, Thomas. *The Role of Medicine: Dream, Mirage, or Nemesis?* 2nd ed. Princeton, NJ: Princeton University Press, 1979.

McKinlay, John B. "A Case for Refocusing Upstream." In *Sociology of Health and Illness: Critical Perspectives*, edited by Peter Conrad and Rochelle Kern, 502–16. 3rd ed. New York: St. Martins, 1990.

McKinlay, John B., and Sonja M. McKinlay. "The Questionable Contribution of Medical Measures to the Decline of Mortality in the United States in the Twentieth Century." *Health and Society* 55, no. 3 (Summer 1977) 405–28.

Merton, Thomas. *Conjectures of a Guilty Bystander.* New York: Image, 1989.

———. *New Seeds of Contemplation.* New York: New Directions, 1961.

———. *No Man Is an Island.* New York: Harcourt Brace Jovanovich, 1978.

Moeller, Susan, et al. "A Day Without Media." Research by ICMPA and students at the Phillip Merrill College of Journalism, University of Maryland. No pages. Online: http://withoutmedia.wordpress.com/.

Nelson, S. Katherine, et al. "In Defense of Parenthood: Children Are Associated With More Joy Than Misery." *Psychological Science* 24, no. 1 (2013) 3–10.

Bibliography

Newport, Frank, et al. "Religious Americans Enjoy Higher Wellbeing." Gallup Wellbeing, February 16, 2012. No pages. Online: http://www.gallup.com/poll/152723/religious-americans-enjoy-higher-wellbeing.aspx.

Nicklas, Jacinda M., et al. "Successful Weight loss Among Obese U.S. Adults." *American Journal of Preventive Medicine* 42, no. 5 (2012) 481–85.

Ogden, Cynthia, and Margaret Carroll, "Prevalence of Obesity Among Children and Adolescents: United States, Trends 1963–1965 Through 2007–2008." Centers for Disease Control and Prevention, Division of Health and Nutrition Examination Surveys. No pages. Online: http://www.cdc.gov/nchs/data/hestat/obesity_child_07_08/obesity_child_07_08.htm.

Palmer, Parker J., and Arthur Zajonc. *The Heart of Higher Education: A Call to Renewal*. San Francisco: Jossey-Bass, 2010.

Peterson, Christopher, and Martin E. P. Seligman. *Character Strengths and Virtues: A Handbook and Classification*. New York: Oxford, 2004.

Peterson, Christopher, Steven F. Maier, and Martin E. P. Seligman. *Learned Helplessness: A Theory for the Age of Personal Control*. New York: Oxford University Press, 1993.

Pope John Paul II. *The Gospel of Life*. New York: Random House, 1995.

Postman, Neil. *Amusing Ourselves to Death*. New York: Penguin, 1985.

Rogers, Will. "President's Organization on Unemployment Relief Broadcast." Speech given on a national radio broadcast with President Herbert Hoover, October 18, 1931.

Rosenhan, David L. "On Being Sane in Insane Places." Online: http://www.bonkersinstitute.org/rosenhan.html.

Rossetti, Stephen J. *When the Lion Roars*. Notre Dame, IN: Ava Maria, 2003.

Russell, A. J., ed. *God Calling: By Two Listeners*. Westwood, NJ: Barbour, 1985.

Saul, John Ralston. *The Doubter's Companion: A Dictionary of Aggressive Common Sense*. New York: Free Press, 1994.

Scheff, T. J. *Being Mentally Ill: A Sociological Theory*. Chicago: Aldine, 1966.

Schlosser, Eric. *Fast Food Nation: The Dark Side of the All-American Meal*. New York: Harper, 2005.

Schwartz, Martin A. "The Importance of Stupidity in Scientific Research." *Journal of Cell Science* 121 (June 1, 2008) 1771.

Scott, Janny, and David Leonhardt. "Shadowy Lines That Still Divide." *New York Times* (May 15, 2005). No pages. Online: http://www

Bibliography

.nytimes.com/2005/05/15/national/class/OVERVIEW-FINAL.html?pagewanted=all.

Seligman, Martin, and Mihaly Csikszentmihalyi. "Positive Psychology: An Introduction." *American Psychologist* 55, no. 1 (2000) 5–14.

Seligman, Martin E. P., and Steven F. Maier. "Failure to Escape Traumatic Shock." *Journal of Experimental Psychology* 74, no. 1 (May 1967) 1–9.

Sheen, Fulton. *Peace of Soul*. Liguori, MO: Liguori, 1949.

———. *Seven Words of Jesus and Mary: Lessons of Cana and Calvary*. New York: Garden City, 1953.

Shrestha, Laura B. "Life Expectancy in the United States." Congressional Research Service Report, The Library of Congress. No pages. Online: http://aging.senate.gov/crs/aging1.pdf.

Sine, Tom. "Branded for Life: 21st Century Global Marketers are More Seductive than Ever Before. And They Want Your Kids." *Sojourners* (September–October 2000). No pages. Online: http://sojo.net/magazine/2000/09/branded-life.

Smith, Christian. "Man the Religious Animal." *First Things* 222 (April 2012) 27–31.

St. Bonaventure University. "Franciscan Values." No pages. Online: http://www.sbu.edu/about_sbu.aspx?id=1858.

Stephens, Mitchell. "Jacques Derrida and Deconstruction." *New York Times Magazine* (January 23, 1994). No pages. Online: http://www.nyu.edu/classes/stephens/Jacques%20Derrida%20-%20NYT%20-%20page.htm.

Stephey, M. J. "A Brief History of: Credit Cards." *Time* (April 23, 2009). No pages. Online: http://www.time.com/time/magazine/article/0,9171,1893507,00.html.

Sykes, Charles J. *The Hollow Men: Politics and Corruption in Higher Education*. Washington, DC: Regnery Gateway, 1990.

Talbot, Strob. "Ethics in the Corporate World." *Time* 129, no. 21 (May 25, 1987) 26–29. Online: http://content.time.com/time/magazine/article/0,9171,964473,00.html

Thier, Dave. "An Estimated 83 Million Facebook Profiles are Fake." *Forbes* (August 2, 2012). No pages. Online: http://www.forbes.com/sites/davidthier/2012/08/02/83-million-estimated-facebook-profiles-are-fake/.

Twenge, Jean M., et al. "Birth Cohort Increases in Psychopathology Among Young Americans, 1938–2007: A Cross-Temporal Meta-Analysis of the MMPI." *Clinical Psychology Review* 30 (2010) 145–54.

Bibliography

United States Army. "Building Resilience Enhancing Performance." Comprehensive Soldier and Family Fitness. No pages. Online: http://csf2.army.mil/index.html.

United States Government. "Federal Debt at the End of Fiscal Year: 1940–2012." Budget of the United States Government, FY 2008, Historical Tables 7.1, 10.1, 13.1. No pages. Online: http://www.econdataus.com/debt08.html.

Viereck, George Sylvester. "What Life Means to Einstein." *Saturday Evening Post* (October 26, 1929). No pages. Online: http://www.saturdayeveningpost.com/wp-content/uploads/satevepost/einstein.pdf.

Wedge, Marilyn. "Why French Kids Don't Have ADHD." *Psychology Today* (March 8, 2012). No Pages. Online: http://www.psychologytoday.com/blog/suffer-the-children/201203/why-french-kids-dont-have-adhd.

Weitz, Rose. "The Social Sources of Modern Illness." In *The Sociology of Health, Illness, and Health Care: A Critical Approach*, 17–47. 6th ed. Boston, MA: Wadsworth, 2013.

White, William L. *Pathways from the Culture of Addiction to the Culture of Recovery*. Center City, MN: Hazelden, 1996.

Worldwatch Institute. "The State of Consumption Today." No pages. Online: http://www.worldwatch.org/node/810.

www.ingramcontent.com/pod-product-compliance
Lightning Source LLC
Chambersburg PA
CBHW072145160426
43197CB00012B/2249